What's Your
FRIENDS
I.Q.?

Good friends. Left to right, Front: Jennifer Aniston,
Matthew Perry, Matt LeBlanc; Rear: David Schwimmer,
Courteney Cox, Lisa Kudrow

What's Your *FRIENDS* I.Q.?

501 Questions and Answers for Fans

STEPHEN SPIGNESI

A CITADEL PRESS BOOK
Published by Carol Publishing Group

A Citadel Press Book
Published by Carol Publishing Group
Citadel Press is a registered trademark of Carol Communications, Inc.
Editorial Offices: 600 Madison Avenue, New York, N.Y. 10022
Sales & Distribution Offices: 120 Enterprise Avenue, Secaucus, N.J.
  07094
In Canada: Canadian Manda Group, P.O. Box 920, Station U, Toronto,
  Ontario M8Z 5P9
Queries regarding rights and permissions should be addressed to
  Carol Publishing Group, 600 Madison Aven''e, New York, N.Y. 10022

Carol Publishing Group books are available at special discounts for
bulk purchases, sales promotion, fund-raising, or educational
purposes. Special editions can be created to specifications. For
details, contact: Special Sales Department, Carol Publishing
Group, 120 Enterprise Avenue, Secaucus, N.J. 07094

Manufactured in the United States of America
10 9 8 7 6 5 4 3 2 1

Library of Congress Cataloging-in-Publication Data

Spignesi, Stephen J.
    What's your friends I.Q.? : 501 questions and answers for fans /
  Stephen Spignesi.
      p.   cm.
    "A Citadel Press book."
    ISBN 0-8065-1776-X
    1. Friends (Television program)—Miscellanea.   I. Title.
  PN1992.77.F76S67   1996
  791.45′72—dc20   95-26391
                                                          CIP

This is for my friend,
Charlie Fried

CONTENTS

PART 1
"I'll Be There for You"

PART 2
The Friends

PART 3
The First Season

PART 4
The Foosball Room

Extras

Answers

INTRODUCTION

> "We all bonded instantly. It's almost scary how well we get along."
>
> —Jennifer "Rachel" Aniston

A few years ago, when I was working on a book about Woody Allen, I repeatedly came across quotes from the Woodman in which he asserted that he never watched TV, except for sports, films, and news. And he also went so far as to express real distaste for network shows. In a *Rolling Stone* interview reprinted in my book, *The Woody Allen Companion*, Woody said:

> *I don't watch what is purported entertainment. I don't watch the junk stuff. I don't find it even remotely rewarding, on any level. It seems to me if I happen to see it while dialing through on the way somewhere, it just looks like elevator music, the height of soulless, plastic, brightly lit, antiseptic, you know . . . stupidity. I don't think it's worth anybody's time.*

Well, guess what?

According to published reports, Woody Allen watches *Friends*.

As do megastars Julia Roberts and Tom Hanks.

And actress Sarah Jessica Parker claims to have seen every single episode.

You know something astonishing is going on when you get this caliber of artist not only admitting to watching a sitcom, but actually going out of his or her way to praise it to the heavens!

And that is what can only be described as the sheer magic of *Friends* first season.

Everything about *Friends* works: It's got a great cast, amazingly good writers, and terrific production values.

At first, *Friends* was criticized as being something "designed" for twentysomethings: Generation Xers. That, as Chandler would say, was so NOT true, that it didn't take long for the show to build up an audience of all age groups and all types of people.

I know a sixty-eight-year-old retired woman who can reel off the jobs and living arrangements of every single Friend.

I know a fourteen-year-old girl who can recite Chandlerisms ad infinitum until you tell her to shut up.

And I am a forty-two-year-old married guy who can relate to and be entertained by the ups and downs in the lives of single people almost twenty years younger.

Why?

Because *Friends* tackles universal subjects in a clever, sensitive, and humorous way.

Even the Marcel the monkey subplot was handled perfectly: In the hands of less talented writers and a less competent cast, it could have easily degenerated into stupid slapstick and boring double entendres.

Friends is one of those perfect TV shows: It has it all, and frankly, shows of this quality don't come around that often on the tube. And its right-out-of-the-gate success is so memorable that we've even included in *What's Your Friends I.Q.?* a final "Last Question" which addresses its quicksilver transformation from just another sitcom to a cultural phenomenon.

So, now it's time to grab a pencil, pour some coffee (what else?), and find out just what YOUR *Friends* I.Q. is!
Enjoy!

New Haven, Connecticut
August 1995

The *Friends* Grading System

What's Your *Friends* I.Q.? consists of 501 questions that test you on your knowledge of all of our Friends, as well as how well you remember what went on in the twenty-four memorable episodes in the first season of the series.

This Grading System will tell you where you score, beginning with the not-too-swift Joey Tribbiani *Latté* Prize and peaking with the ultimate Ross Geller *Iced Tea* Trophy. (And by the way, these awards have all been carefully designed based on the favorite beverages of the Friend for whom they are named.)

Number of Correct Answers	The Friends *Award*
0–50	**The Joey Tribbiani *Latté* Prize**
51–100	**The Phoebe Buffay *Soda With Thumb* Honor**
101–200	**The Rachel Green *Coffee Decaf* Citation**
201–300	**The Monica Geller *Decaf Cappuccino* Memorial**
301–400	**The Chandler Bing *Coffee Black* Award**
401–501	**The Ross Geller *Iced Tea* Trophy**

THE *FRIENDS* REFRESHER COURSE:
FIVE COMMONLY ASKED QUESTIONS

1. What is *Friends* about?

Friends's executive producers Kevin Bright, Marta Kauffman and David Crane described the series as "about love, sex, careers and a time in life when everything is possible. It's about searching for commitment and security—and a fear of commitment and security. And, most of all, it's a show about friendship—because when a person is young and single in the city, friends and family are synonymous."

2. Who are the *Friends*?

NBC's *Friends* press release from September 1994, (the month the show premiered), introduced the lovable sextet thusly:

At the center of this group is Monica, a bright woman with a knack for meeting the wrong men. An assistant chef at an uptown restaurant, she has had to work for everything—unlike Rachel, her pampered best friend from high school.

As Monica's new roomate, Rachel is embarking on a life of independence after having left her fiancé at the altar.

Monica's older brother, Ross, was thrust into bachelorhood when his wife announced she was a lesbian and left

him. A hopeless romantic, he misses married life and fears
there might have only been one woman in the world for him.

Across the hall from Monica are Chandler and Joey.

Chandler, a wry observer of everyone's life, is romanti-
cally detached and professionally unmotivated.

Joey, a struggling actor, is more passionate about life.
He loves women, sports, New York and most of all, himself.

Rounding out the circle of friends is Monica's former
college roommate, Phoebe, an off-beat, eternally optimistic
waif.

3. How did the *Friends* meet?

When asked this question on the *Friends* Internet news-
group, supervising producer Jeff Greenstein gave what he
described as the "quasi-definitive" answer ("as we writer
folk have discussed it over the course of the season," he
explained):

In the pilot, we established that Monica, Rachel and Ross
all went to Lincoln High School together.

Rachel and Monica were close, but they drifted [apart]—
enough so that Rachel didn't invite Monica to her wedding.
We also established that Ross had a crush on Rachel back
then.

[At one point], Schwimmer and Perry wondered if Chandler and Ross might have gone to college together. We writers agreed that it might be nice for two of our other characters to have a history together, so we wrote it in.

Therefore, my guess is that when Monica graduated college and was looking for an apartment, Chandler . . . alerted
her to the fact that an apartment was opening up across the
hall from him. Monica found Phoebe through a roommate-
matching service and moved in.

When Chandler's roommate Kip got married, he moved

out and Joey (who Chandler probably also met through a roommate-matching service, or by putting up flyers at the laundromat) moved in.

Around the same time, Phoebe's grandmother needed some kind of taking care of, so Phoebe moved out of Monica's to live with her.

4. What did the show's cast and creative team do before *Friends*?

Friends executive producers KEVIN BRIGHT, MARTA KAUFFMAN and DAVID CRANE were the executive producers of HBO's smash hit *Dream On*.

JENNIFER ANISTON's film credits include *Leprechaun* and *The Edge*. Her TV credits include appearances on the series *Ferris Bueller*, *The Edge*, and *Muddling Through*.

COURTENEY COX's film credits include *Ace Ventura: Pet Detective*, *Sketch Artist II: Hands that See*, *Blue Desert*, *Mr. Destiny*, *Roxanne: The Prize Pulitzer*, *Cocoon: The Return*, *I'll Be Home for Christmas*, *If It's Tuesday, It Still Must Be Belgium*, *Masters of the Universe*, and *Misfits of Science*. Her TV credits include appearances on the series *Family Ties* and *Misfits of Science*. Cox was also the girl that Bruce Springsteen pulled out of the audience in his video "Dancing in the Dark."

LISA KUDROW's film credits include *The Unborn* and *In the Heat of Passion*. Her TV credits include appearances on the series *Newhart*, *Coach*, and *Mad About You*, in which she has a recurring role as Phoebe's twin sister, Ursula.

MATT LEBLANC's film credits include *Lookin' Italian*, and *Anything to Survive*. His TV credits include appearances on *Married With Children*, *Red Shoe Diaries*, *Top of the Heap*, and *TV 101*.

MATTHEW PERRY's film credits include *Deadly Relations*,

She's Out of Control, and *Dance 'Til Dawn*. His TV credits include appearances on *Home Free*, *Beverly Hills, 90210*, *Sydney*, *Charles in Charge*, and *Growing Pains*.

DAVID SCHWIMMER's film credits include *Twenty Bucks*, *Crossing the Bridge*, *Flight of the Intruder*, and *The Pallbearer*. His TV credits include appearances on *The Wonder Years*, *NYPD Blue*, and *Monty*.

5. In the show's theme song, are the Rembrandts singing "So no one told you THAT was gonna be this way" or "So no one told you LIFE was gonna be this way"?

Life.

Part 1

"I'll Be There for You"

I'll Be There for You.

FRIENDS FUNDAMENTALS

This "Fundamentals" quiz tests your knowledge of basic *Friends* details and info.

1 According to the Friends, dating has its own special language. Match the *spoken* sentiment from the left column with its *real* meaning from the right column:

A. "We should do this again."

B. "It's not you."

C. "You're such a nice guy."

D. "I think we should see other people."

1. "It *is* you."

2. "Ha, ha, I already am."

3. "You will never see me naked."

4. "I'm gonna be dating leather-wearing alcoholics and complaining about them to you."

2 What high school did Rachel, Ross, and Monica all attend?

3 How many bedrooms are there in Monica and Rachel's apartment?

4 What was the name of Chandler's assistant at work?

A. Ellen

B. Helen

C. Kelly

5 Why do the Friends call the ugly naked guy who lives across the way from Monica and Rachel "Ugly Naked Guy"?

6 Which of the following teas are available at the coffee-house where the Friends meet after work?
  A. Earl Grey
  B. English Breakfast
  C. Cinnamon Stick
  D. Chamomile
  E. Mint Medley
  F. Blackberry
  G. Lemon Soother
  H. Atomic Zinger
  I. All of the above

7 How did Ross acquire Marcel the monkey?
  A. Ross bought him from a zoo that was going bankrupt.
  B. Ross bribed a circus guy.
  C. Ross's friend Bethel rescued him from a lab.

8 What is the name of the restaurant where Monica works as a chef?
  A. Chez Lenny
  B. Iridium
  C. Belize

9 TOO EASY?: What is the name of the coffeehouse where Rachel works, Phoebe sings, and everyone else just hangs out?

10 TOO HARD?: What was the number of Monica and Rachel's apartment in the *Friends* pilot and second episode *only*?

    A. 5

    B. 6

    C. 7

11 What was the number of Monica and Rachel's apartment for the rest of the season?

    A. 19

    B. 20

    C. 21

12 Who is "Satan in a smock"?

    A. Paolo, according to Rachel

    B. Paul the Wine Guy, according to Monica

    C. Barry, according to Rachel

13 What is the number of Joey and Chandler's apartment?

    A. 19

    B. 20

    C. 21

14 TRUE OR FALSE: Monica gets the *New York Times* delivered.

15 CROSSOVER DREAMS: Why did Phoebe's sister Ursula work at Riff's?

    A. Because it was close to where she lived and the aprons were really cute.

    B. Because the owner's brother once bought her cousin Gloria's Saab.

C. Because one of the waitresses once worked for a
caterer that did Madonna and Sean Penn's wedding
reception.

16 Who was Chandler speaking to when he said, "You are
one of the most caring, most responsible men in North
America"?
  A. Joey
  B. Ross
  C. His boss, Mr. Douglas, in a shameless attempt at
  sucking up.

17 TOUGH ONE: What was the number of Mr. Heckles's
apartment?
  A. 8
  B. 9
  C. 10

18 Exactly how far is it from Chandler and Joey's apartment
to the coffeehouse?
  A. Ninety-seven steps
  B. One-tenth of a mile and three stairs
  C. One-and-a-third football fields

19 TOUGH ONE: What was the name of the guy who owned
the coffeehouse?
  A. Geraldo
  B. José
  C. Arturo

20 TRUE OR FALSE: Ross and Monica's Aunt Sylvia was married to Uncle Freddy.

21 Which of the Friends did Phoebe once describe as "floopy"?

    A. Monica

    B. Rachel

    C. Joey

22 Who once asked Rachel for a piece of that "wonderful, nutty, chocolatey, kind of kinky pie thing"?

    A. Ross

    B. Joey

    C. Chandler

23 According to Phoebe, whose haircut did baby Ben have?

    A. Carol's

    B. Monica's

    C. Ross's

24 What was the name of the laundromat where Monica and Rachel did their laundry?

    A. Suds 'R' Us

    B. Launderama

    C. Stop 'n' Soap

25 According to Ross, which vacuum cleaner attachment was the one that no one knew what it was used for? (And about which, we are not supposed to ask, for that matter?)

    A. The long one with the flat end

    B. The short, wedge-shaped one

    C. The round one with the bristles

26 TRUE OR FALSE: The blackout that stranded Chandler darkened all of Manhattan and parts of Brooklyn and Queens.

27 Where, exactly, did Rachel first meet Paolo?
   A. At a gym
   B. At the coffeehouse
   C. In the hallway of their apartment building during the blackout

28 How do the Friends get out onto the balcony off Monica and Rachel's apartment?

29 What was Monica and Ross's affectionate nickname for their grandfather?
   A. Pop-Pop
   B. Gramps
   C. Poppie

30 TRUE OR FALSE: Carol's Susan is a vegetarian.

31 Chandler and his "pre-Joey" roommate chipped in and bought a certain piece of cooking equipment together. What did they buy?
   A. A frying pan
   B. A microwave oven
   C. A Hibachi

32 TRUE OR FALSE: Joey's dad wore a hairpiece.

33 Why was Monica shunned by the Amish?
   A. Because she bought a pair of pants with a zipper.
   B. Because she bought a blow dryer.

C. Because she got caught using gel in her hair.

34 TRUE OR FALSE: Around the time Monica was dating Ethan, the coffeehouse had new hand dryers installed in the bathrooms.

35 Who is "Carol's ex-husband's sister's roommate"?

Part 2

The Friends

The father of the Chandlerism.

CHANDLER BING

Chandler is the wittiest of a *very* witty bunch. Vocal and sardonic, his one-liners often slay his pals and paint a picture of a guy who is confident and positive, but . . . we all know better about our pal, Chan, now don't we?

36 How old was Chandler when his parents told him they were getting divorced?

37 TRUE OR FALSE: In a five month period, Chandler dumped Janice three times.

38 What did Janice have printed on the candy hearts she had made especially for Chandler?
   A. "Jan & Chan 4-Ever"
   B. "Reunited"
   C. "I Am Your Destiny"
   D. "Call Me"

39 Chandler's job required close attention to something called the W.E.N.U.S. What does W.E.N.U.S. mean? (BLOOPER ALERT and HINT: The answer to this question can be found in the episode "The One With the Stoned Guy" [which guest starred Jon Lovitz]. In it, Matthew Perry accidentally said "Systems" instead of "Statistics" for the last word when he explained the term to the Friends but because the laugh came as soon as he said the word "W.E.N.U.S.," the director decided to let it go.)

40 What type of high school did Chandler attend?

    A. A rundown inner city school.

    B. An elite, co-ed suburban high school.

    C. A boarding school with 400 boys.

41 TRUE OR FALSE: Chandler always welled up when the Grinch's heart expanded in the Dr. Seuss story and broke the measuring device.

42 Chandler once had a dream in which his genitals were replaced by a ringing telephone. During his dream, who called him on his new "equipment"?

    A. His mother, which was a real surprise: "She *never* calls me."

    B. MCI. They wanted him to join Family and Friends 2.

    C. Some guy who wanted to know what he was wearing.

43 COMPLETE THE CHANDLERISM: Once when discussing Ross's lesbian ex-wife Chandler made the following remark, which he followed with "Did I say that *out loud*?!" "Sometimes I wish I was a _____ ."

44 Chandler once had a dream in which he was which female singer in Las Vegas?

    A. Bette Midler

    B. Barbra Streisand

    C. Liza Minnelli

45 TRUE OR FALSE: As a child, Chandler had an imaginary friend his parents actually preferred over him.

46 How long had Chandler *not* smoked when he started again around the time Phoebe got the free money from the bank?

  A. one year
  B. three years
  C. five years

47 According to Chandler, what serial killer did Ross look like with his "dented face" bandages?

48 What was the name of the Italian girl Chandler met at a performance of Joey's musical *Freud!*?

  A. Andromeda
  B. Agnes
  C. Aurora

49 TRUE OR FALSE: Chandler was especially proud of the fact that he actually once rode the subway alone to Brooklyn at night.

50 Whom did Chandler fantasize about calling when model Jill Goodacre asked him if he wanted to use her phone during the blackout?

  A. Every girl in his life who had ever said "no" to him when he had asked them to dance.
  B. *The National Enquirer*
  C. About 300 guys he went to high school with.

51 Why did Chandler initially refuse the piece of gum offered to him by Jill Goodacre?

  A. Because it was sugarless
  B. Because it wasn't sugarless

52 What animal once bit Chandler at the zoo?

    A. A monkey

    B. A tiger

    C. A peacock

53 Who is Big Al?

54 What was Chandler choking on when Jill Goodacre Heimliched him in the ATM vestibule?

    A. Someone else's gum

    B. A peanut

    C. The top of a Bic pen

55 RIDICULOUSLY OBSCURE QUESTION: What was the number of Chandler's checking account?

56 TRUE OR FALSE: In college, Ross once told a girl that Chandler was dating a guy named Bernie Spellman.

57 On what TV show did Chandler's mom reveal that she had bought him his first condoms?

    A. *The Tonight Show* with Jay Leno

    B. *Late Night* with Conan O'Brien

    C. *The Late Show* with David Letterman

58 What was the name of Chandler's roommate before Joey?

    A. Kip

    B. Skip

    C. Chip

59 TRUE OR FALSE: Chandler is an only child.

60 What fortune-telling artifact did Chandler keep on his desk?

    A. A Ouija board.

    B. A single, unopened fortune cookie ("for emergencies").

    C. A Magic 8 Ball.

61 TRUE OR FALSE: Chandler did a killer Stevie Wonder impression.

62 Around the time that Ross's son Ben was born, how much did Chandler say Joey owed him?

    A. The national debt of Nairobi

    B. Seventeen jillion dollars

    C. A gillion dollars

63 According to Chandler, how do real men put out barbecue fires?

    A. Real men just let them burn until they "pitifully whither from a lack of oxygen."

    B. They slam them with the garden hose and "let the ashes fall where they may."

    C. They pee on them, "no get invited back."

64 What did Chandler give Rachel for her birthday during the party that Ross had to leave because of his trip to China?

    A. Travel Scrabble

    B. A Dr. Seuss book

    C. A cameo brooch

65 THINK ABOUT IT: How did Chandler attempt to "turn back time" after he blurted out that Ross was in love with Rachel?

PHOEBE BUFFAY

Phoebe is the New Agey, Earth Child, Vegetarian Masseuse of the Friends, a faux airhead who often sees more than the rest of them all put together. (Even if her observations do come from a slightly skewed perspective!) Phoebe is into aura cleansing and writes incredibly strange folk songs. Answer the following questions about the enigmatic Ms. Buffay.

66 What was Phoebe the vegetarian's philosophy regarding food?

    A. "No food that ever had a mother."

    B. "No food that I could have once named if I had wanted to."

    C. "No food with a face."

67 Which butt cheek did Phoebe get shot in while trying to protect Marcel from a tranquilizer dart?

    A. Right

    B. Left

68 What type of potatoes did Phoebe insist on having for Thanksgiving dinner?

    A. Whipped with peas and onions

    B. French fries

    C. Tater tots

69 TRUE OR FALSE: According to Phebes, she could not wear a digital watch because she was a magnet.

70 With which of her relatives did Phoebe live?
   A. Her mother
   B. Her grandmother
   C. Her twin sister Ursula

71 TRUE OR FALSE: One of the songs in Phoebe's original repertoire was about a snowman.

72 Phoebe once wrote a song about the urn in which she kept her mother's ashes (and "even her eyelashes"). What color was this receptacle?

73 Who walked first, Phoebe or her sister Ursula?

74 What precious possession of Phoebe's did Ursula once break by throwing it under a bus?
   A. Her E-Z Bake Oven
   B. Her Judy Jetson thermos
   C. Her Malibu Barbie Play Set

75 Phoebe once dated a guy named Carl who had a particularly peculiar habit. What was it?
   A. He shaved his eyebrows.
   B. He ate chalk.
   C. He was a ventriloquist who would only speak through his dummy, Earl.

76 What did Phoebe once do to herself that caused her to remark fearfully, "That can't be good!"
   A. She swallowed some lipstick.

  B. She mistakenly used oregano instead of lavender dur-
     ing an aromatherapy session.
  C. She pulled out four of her own eyelashes.

77 TRUE OR FALSE: One of Phoebe's "special skills" was
reading people's feet.

78 How old was Phoebe when she first moved to New York?
  A. Fourteen
  B. Eighteen
  C. Twenty-one

79 To whom did Phoebe give the extra money and free gift
her bank mistakenly gave her?
  A. Monica
  B. Lizzie the homeless woman
  C. David the Physicist Guy

80 How much did the soda company give Phoebe for the
thumb she found in her soda?
  A. $1,000
  B. $5,000
  C. $7,000

81 TRUE OR FALSE: Phoebe did both herbal and Shiatsu mas-
sages.

82 What tragedy happened on the day Phoebe got her first
paycheck?
  A. Jim Morrison died.
  B. There was a cave-in at the mine and eight people
     were killed.
  C. Mount St. Helens erupted.

83 TRUE OR FALSE: Before Chandler hired Phoebe, she was considering going to work operating a drill press.

84 What was Phoebe's first job?
   A. She worked at a Dairy Queen.
   B. She washed car windows outside the Port Authority.
   C. She was a phone sex operator.

85 TRUE OR FALSE: Another one of Phoebe's "special skills" was reading people's palms.

86 FILL-IN-THE-BLANK: When Chandler asked if people thought he was gay because of his hair, Phoebe replied, "Yes, you have _____ hair."

87 What was the single most important thing in Phoebe's life?
   A. Her aromatherapy treatments
   B. Her friends
   C. Her songs

88 TRUE OR FALSE: Phoebe once dated a puppeteer.

89 How did Phoebe get even with Steve the Restaurant Guy for ruining Monica's "dinner audition"?
   A. She made Rachel give him extra-strong caffeinated coffee (when all he was supposed to drink was decaf).
   B. She dug her elbows into him during his next massage.
   C. She put a curse on all the parsley in his new restaurant.

90 THE QUESTION WITH THE BUILT-IN HINT: What video game was Phoebe playing when she suggested "Flameboy" to Joey as a cool stage name?

91 COMPLETE THE LYRICS: Fill in the missing words from this song Phoebe sang in the hospital waiting room while Carol was in labor:

> "They're tiny and chubby and so _____ to touch,
> And soon they'll grow up and _____ you so much."

92 Which of the following facts about Phoebe's life are true?

A. Her father left home when she was young.

B. Her mother committed suicide when she was a kid.

C. Her stepfather ended up in jail.

D. All of the above.

93 How did Phoebe colorfully describe hamburger meat?

A. "The ground-up flesh of formerly cute cows and turkeys."

B. "The solemn remains of our bovine friends."

C. "Plastic-wrapped containers of too many lost moos."

94 What was Phoebe talking about when she told the others that she didn't think any of their lives would ever be the same again?

A. She was talking about Chandler's promotion.

B. She was talking about the revelation that Ross was in love with Rachel.

C. She was talking about Paolo's pass at her.

95 According to Phoebe, how many dates did a couple have to have before they were in a "relationshipy place"?

A. Five

B. Ten

C. Fifteen

MONICA GELLER

Monica is wound awfully tight, but it's really not her fault. Her mother did to her what her grandmother did to Monica's mother, and so on, and so on, going back generations. But still, Monica is great fun (Her "You suck!" to Chandler during an especially spirited game of Foosball was a high point of my life) and her apartment (which she shares with Rachel) is often the meeting place for the six Friends. (Aside from the coffeehouse, of course.) Answer the following questions about the incredibly tidy Ms. Geller.

96 According to her father, which of the following were true about Monica as a child?

    A. She was chubby.

    B. She had no friends.

    C. She always read in her room.

    D. She liked to do puzzles.

    E. All of the above.

97 TRUE OR FALSE: Monica was invited to Rachel's interrupted wedding.

98 What piece of living room furniture did Monica never want moved (and which Rachel decided one day to relocate)?

    A. The white rocker

Monica, in her "pre–Dudley Moore" phase. (That's a second-season reference, by the way. But you already knew that, right?)

    B. The blue loveseat

    C. The green ottoman

99 Monica's dad had a special nickname for her that had a "musical" ring to it, if you know what I mean. What was it?

100 Monica once dated a guy named Steve who had a certain speech impediment. What was it?

  A. He lisped.

  B. He stuttered.

  C. He couldn't say the letter "L."

101 What musical did Monica appear in in high school as "an Alp"? (HINT: Chandler saw a yearbook picture of Monica in the musical standing in front of a bunch of kids and cracked that he thought she was "an Alp.")

  A. *Freud!*

  B. *The Sound of Music*

  C. *On a Clear Day You Can See Forever*

102 Why did Monica call her ex-boyfriend Howard the "I Win Guy"?

  A. Because he would chant "I win, you lose" in a sing-songy voice every time he beat her in Monopoly.

  B. Because he always had to finish eating first when they were out in a restaurant, after which he would slam down his fork and exclaim, "I win!"

  C. Because he would shout "I win!" every time he had an orgasm.

103 TRUE OR FALSE: Monica had a picture of her hairy ex-boyfriend Scotty Jarred naked.

104 TRUE OR FALSE: Monica was really skinny in high school.

105 Paul the Wine Guy gave Monica a line (which he also used on her coworker Franny) to get Mon into bed. What was it?

A. He told her that he hadn't been able to have sex for
   two years because a girl dumped him and broke his
   heart.
B. He told her he had six weeks to live.
C. He told her he was in the CIA and was soon going
   away "for a very long time" on a top secret mission.

106 Monica once went out with one of Joey's cousins, a guy
who could do something disgusting with the alphabet. What
was this gentleman's particular "skill"?

107 Which of the following questions did Monica ask
Rachel when Rachel told her she wasn't sure if she wanted
to date Ross?
A. Isn't he cute enough?
B. Doesn't he make enough money?
C. Is there someone else?
D. All of the above

108 TRUE OR FALSE: When Monica was a kid, her Raggedy
Ann doll was the raggediest one in the neighborhood.

109 Which of the following were absolute "musts" for Monica?
A. She had to pay all her bills right away.
B. She had to have the laundry detergent with the e-z
   pour spout.
C. She insisted on using coasters for all beverages.
D. All of the above.

110 According to Monica, what was it about Chandler that
made people think he was gay?

    A. She said he had "an air about him."

    B. She said no straight man could put together an outfit like Chandler.

    C. She said he had "a quality."

111 What "whipped fish" creation did Monica make Joey taste before her "dinner audition" with Steve the Restaurant Guy?

    A. Shrimp gelatiné

    B. Crab and spinach roulade

    C. Salmon mousse

112 Why did the maternally-yearning Monica burst into tears while talking to her mother from the hospital waiting room while Carol was in labor?

113 How much was Monica planning on paying Wendy, her original waitress for her "dinner audition" with Steve the Restaurant Guy?

    A. $10 an hour

    B. $12 an hour

    C. $20 an hour

114 How much did Monica end up paying Rachel, her *actual* "dinner audition" waitress?

    A. $10 an hour

    B. $12 an hour

    C. $20 an hour

115 TOUGH ONE: How much did Monica spend on the Wonder Mop?

    A. $69.95

    B. $79.95
    C. $89.95

116 What was Monica's "Pennsylvania Dutch" alias?

117 What basketball team had taken over the whole sixth floor of the hotel that Monica and Fake Monica tried to crash one day by pretending they were the Gunnersons in Room 615?
    A. The New York Knicks
    B. The Boston Celtics
    C. The Chicago Bulls

118 TRUE OR FALSE: Monica would enthusiastically recommend the movie *Mrs. Doubtfire* to friends.

119 How old was Monica when she dated Ethan the virgin?
    A. Twenty-four
    B. Twenty-five
    C. "Twenty-five and thirteen months"

120 The first time Monica held her nephew Ben, she made him a solemn promise. What was it?
    A. "I will always have gum."
    B. "I will always have your favorite cereal in my cabinet."
    C. "I will always help you with your Halloween costume."

121 When Ross went to China, what did he ask Monica to do so that Ben wouldn't forget him?
    A. To show Ben his picture now and then.

    B. To whisper "Daddy's coming back" in his ear when he was sleeping, every day until he returned.

    C. To tell the baby that Susan wasn't his real father when Carol and Susan weren't looking.

122 What did Monica suggest to Joey as an alternative when he couldn't have normal sex because of the fertility study he was participating in?

123 In an attempt to weasel an answer out of Rachel about her feelings for Ross, what did Monica offer to save for her at the conclusion of her birthday party?

    A. The box Ross's gift came in.

    B. The plastic fork she was using when she learned that Ross was in love with her.

    C. The wrapping paper Ross's gift was in.

124 What was Monica talking about when she excitedly told Rachel, "We'd be like Friends-in-Laws!"?

125 What did Monica give Rachel for her birthday that Rachel ended up exchanging for a skirt?

    A. A blouse

    B. A pair of sneakers

    C. A sweatsuit

David "Ross Geller" Schwimmer in his pre-*Friends* days as "Greg Richardson" on the shortlived 1993 series, *Monty*. (PHOTOFEST/PHOTO BY CHARLES BUSH)

Ross Geller

Ross is hyper-intelligent, a voracious reader, and an impeccably precise speaker, but all his romantic relationships have been cataclysmically disastrous. He thought he had found true love with Carol, his ex-wife, but that didn't work out. And at the end of the first season, we were all still waiting to see if his unrequited love for Rachel becomes requited, if you know what I mean. Ross is Monica's brother and they are fiercely close. Answer the following questions about the very specific Mr. Geller.

126 What is Ross's profession?

A. He's a marine biologist.

B. He's a paleontologist.

C. He's a software salesman.

127 How did Ross like his mashed potatoes?

A. With lumps

B. "Creamy and smooth"

C. With peas and onions

128 What did Ross's ex-wife Carol do for a living?

A. She was a writer.

B. She was a paleontologist.

C. She taught sixth grade.

129 What exactly was Ross suggesting when he said, "Let's try scooching"?

130 What were the first words Ross ever said to his unborn child during his first episode of "belly time?"
   A. "Hello, baby."
   B. "Aloha, big guy."
   C. "Anybody home?"

131 What term did Ross's ex-wife Carol and her new significant other Susan prefer when describing their relationship?
   A. "life companion"
   B. "spousal partner"
   C. "life partner"

132 TRUE OR FALSE: Ross wore a mechanical watch. (HINT: The answer to this question can be found in the "Birth" episode during a competitive contraction timing contest between Ross and Susan.)

133 While they were having dinner together in a restaurant, Ross's dad remarked that he wished he had a piece of a certain "salad-related" business. What business was Jack Geller talking about?
   A. The marinated artichoke hearts business.
   B. The sun-dried tomato business.
   C. The pimento business. ("Just think about all those empty olives out there!")

134 TRUE OR FALSE: The first time Ross's dad really felt like a Dad was when one-day-old Ross grabbed his finger.

135 What New Age ritual did Phoebe attempt to perform on Ross when she learned that his wife had left him for another woman?

> A. She started to read the bumps on his head but Ross stopped her.
>
> B. She tried to cleanse his aura.
>
> C. She chanted over his third chakra because "the first two wouldn't do diddly to balance someone rejected by a lesbian."

136 During a Friends poker game, who did Ross once call "The Big Green Poker Machine"?

137 Using the "grabbing a spoon" metaphor as a way of describing dating, Ross told Joey and Chandler he hadn't grabbed a spoon since which certain pop song was being played on the radio?

> A. "Billy, Don't Be a Hero"
>
> B. "Summer in the City"
>
> C. "Sunshine Superman"

138 TRUE OR FALSE: Ross got hit in the face with a hockey puck at a Rangers-Penguins game.

139 What was the exact name of the museum where Ross worked?

> A. The Museum of Prehistoric Artifacts
>
> B. The Museum of Prehistory
>
> C. The Museum of Prehistoric History

140 TRUE OR FALSE: Ross's dog ChiChi was sent to the Milners' farm in Connecticut to live when Ross was a kid.

141 What name did Ross suggest to Carol and Susan if their baby was a girl?

    A. Janice

    B. Julia

    C. Minnie

142 TRUE OR FALSE: Ross could fall asleep in a public place anytime he felt like it.

143 Why was October 20 so important to Ross?

    A. It was the day he got Marcel.

    B. It was the day he and Carol first had sex (and he lost his virginity).

    C. It was the day ChiChi was taken away.

144 TRUE OR FALSE: The first time Ross and Carol made love, she was barefoot, which was a major turn-on for Mr. Geller.

145 What was Ross's bicycling magazine of choice?

    A. *Spokes*

    B. *Cycling*

    C. *Bikes*

146 TRUE OR FALSE: Ross usually used Downy fabric softener.

147 After decades of looking, where did Ross finally find his retainer?

    A. In Nana's closet

    B. Under the bureau in his old room

    C. In a cigar box in his father's garage

148 What was Ross's worst fear?

149 COMPLETE ROSS'S BOAST: "You could plunk me down in the middle of any woman's _____ , no compass, and I could find my way out of there like that."

150 Ross once dated a young lady named Celia that the others sarcastically called "The Bug Lady." Why did they call her this?

    A. Because her great-grandfather was famous for correctly identifying the length of a gnat's sperm.

    B. Because she had this peculiar habit of swatting away invisible mosquitoes when she talked.

    C. Because she was the Curator of Insects at the museum where Ross worked.

151 FILL-IN-THE-FAMOUS AUTHOR'S NAME: After Ross successfully talked dirty to Celia, he told Joey he was the _____ of dirty talk. (HINT: He said he utilized characters, plot lines, themes, motifs, and even villagers during his dirty talking crusade.)

152 Ross once dated a girl named Linda who believed something about *The Flintstones* that left Ross shaking his head in astonishment. What did the anthropologically-challenged Linda believe?

153 On first seeing his son Ben, Ross said he looked like his Uncle Ed covered in a certain food substance. What food did Ross mention?

    A. Pudding

    B. A-1 Sauce

    C. Jell-O

154 FILL-IN-THE-BLANK: Before Ross went to China, he explained the trip to Monica and Phoebe by telling them, "It's a whole _____ thing."

155 What expensive figurine did Ross buy for Carol when he fell in love with her back in college?

    A. A crystal wizard

    B. A crystal horse

    C. A crystal duck

RACHEL GREEN

Rachel is a great date. She knows how to dress, loves to party, and is usually the *life* of the party. She comes from privilege and gets her kicks out of spending money, but after leaving her fiancé at the altar, she had to learn how to get by on a waitress's pay. Rachel rooms with Monica and is on occasion woefully naive about life in the real world. But she makes a great dip and looks terrific in Italian shoes! Answer these questions about the fetching Ms. Green.

156 TRUE OR FALSE: Rachel usually spent every Thanksgiving with her family skiing in Vail, Colorado.

157 Who taught Rachel how to kiss?

158 Why did Rachel call her ex-boyfriend Pete Carney "Pete the Weeper"?

    A. Because he cried every time he saw her.

    B. Because he cried every time they had sex.

    C. Because he cried every time he saw *Terms of Endearment*.

159 What is Rachel's middle name?

160 TRUE OR FALSE: Rachel and Mindy went to camp together.

161 Rachel once shared the fact that by their sixth date Paolo had done something unique to her breasts. What had the Italian gigolo done to her boobies?

A. Anointed them with olive oil.

B. Photographed them. Individually.

C. Named them.

162 TRUE OR FALSE: Rachel had Blue Cross medical insurance.

163 Which of the following is Rachel's sweetener of choice?

A. Equal

B. Sweet & Low

C. Sugar

164 TRUE OR FALSE: According to Luisa Giannetti, the Animal Control Agent, Rachel was a bitch in high school.

165 Before she moved in with Monica, who paid Rachel's charge card bills?

A. Her father

B. Her fiancé Barry

C. Her mother

166 How much did Rachel's called-off wedding cost her father?

A. $10,000

B. $20,000

C. $40,000

167 Rachel's dad once offered her an automobile if she would leave New York and come home. What kind of car did he offer her?

    A. A Corvette
    B. A Mercedes convertible
    C. A Lexus

168 TRUE OR FALSE: Rachel was generally so timid, she couldn't even send back soup.

169 Who gave Rachel the shoes she wore to Nana's funeral?
    A. Paolo
    B. Ross
    C. Her father

170 Where do you usually find niffles?

171 Rachel's sister had a vacation place which she let Rachel and Paolo use one weekend. Where was this place?
    A. In the Catskills
    B. In the Poconos
    C. In the New Hampshire woods

172 What did Rachel tell Chandler she *could* see through his shirt when he returned home from his Career Counseling tests?
    A. His sleeveless T-shirt
    B. His "Mother" tattoo
    C. His nipples

173 Two things Rachel hated about being a waitress were lousy tips and being called a certain name. What was that name?
    A. "Excuse me?"
    B. "Waitress"
    C. "Missy?"

174 TRUE OR FALSE: Rachel had "excellent compuper skills."

175 To what "popular" magazine did Rachel send a résumé during her job-hunting blitz?
   A. *Popular Styles*
   B. *People*
   C. *Popular Mechanics*

176 TRUE OR FALSE: Rachel was a horrible tap dancer.

177 When Carol and Susan were late getting to the hospital for the birth of Ben, Rachel attempted to make a "Chandleresque" joke about having the baby in a cab and how much the labor and delivery would cost. What "prices" did she assign to the contractions?
   A. One dollar for the first contraction and twenty-five cents for each additional.
   B. Two dollars for the first contraction and fifty cents for each additional.
   C. Three dollars for the first contraction and seventy-five cents for each additional.

178 What did Rachel's father do for a living?
   A. He was a doctor.
   B. He was an airline pilot.
   C. He was a mortician.

179 Where did Rachel meet Carl?
   A. At the gym
   B. At Chandler's office
   C. At the coffeehouse

180 What actor and his electric car really aggravated Rachel's dimwitted date Carl?

181 What did Joey's new girlfriend Melanie give Rachel for her birthday?

    A. A fruit basket

    B. Travel Scrabble

    C. A gift certificate for coffee

182 Who shouted at Rachel, "I love you! Deal with me first!" as she was leaving for the airport to see Ross after learning of his true feelings for her?

    A. Carl

    B. Joey

    C. Chandler

183 TRUE OR FALSE: Rachel was able to successfully get a message to Ross before he left for China.

184 How did Rachel learn that Ross had been in love with her since the ninth grade?

    A. Chandler told her that, too.

    B. Ross came to her in a daydream and told her.

    C. Monica told her.

185 What did Rachel bring to the airport as a gift for Ross when he returned from China?

    A. Flowers

    B. Her high school class ring

    C. A bottle of champagne and two glasses

JOEY TRIBBIANI

Is our Joey *really* as dimwitted as he sometimes seems to be? Yes and no. Every now and then Joey comes out with a remark that is insightful and clever, enough so that the others actually stop in mid-sentence to look at him. But then there are those times when he's as dense as an ottoman. Whatever the case, though, Joey is lovable and cute and his friends adore him. Answer the following questions about the impish Signore Tribbiani.

186 What cologne did Joey once spritz on people in a department store?

    A. Eternity

    B. Brut

    C. Aramis

187 What type of potatoes did Joey insist on having for Thanksgiving dinner?

    A. French fries

    B. Potatoes au gratin (with *two* cheeses)

    C. Tater tots

188 TRUE OR FALSE: Joey did not like nudity in movies. He preferred a good story over sexy scenes.

189 Which of the following foods did Joey say he cooked naked?

A. Toast

B. Oatmeal

C. Bacon

190 TRUE OR FALSE: Joey's exercise regimen consisted mainly of free weights.

191 How did Joey describe his high school years?

A. "The worst six years of my life."

B. "Babe Heaven."

C. "Four years of parties, dating, and sex."

192 Joey once appeared in a Wee One's production of a certain classic fable. Name it.

A. *Little Red Riding Hood*

B. *Pinocchio*

C. *Rumpelstiltskin*

193 What was the name of the character Joey played in the prison drama he rehearsed with Chandler?

A. Devin

B. Darrell

C. Damone

194 TRUE OR FALSE: During a discussion with his dad about his dad's mistress, Joey admitted to having been in love ten times.

195 Usually, how many auditions a month did Joey go on?

A. None

B. Three

C. Thirty

196 During the blackout, why did Joey tell Monica that Ross was planning a surprise birthday party for her?

197 Why did Ross once call Joey "Rabbi Tribbiani"?
- A. Because he brought a lit Hanukkah menorah to Monica's apartment during the blackout.
- B. Because Ross once saw him snacking on gefilte fish during *Love Connection*.
- C. Because Ross once caught him wearing Chandler's former roommate's yarmulke to keep the dust off his hair when he was vacuuming.

198 TRUE OR FALSE: Joey never found out that Monica had a crush on him when he moved into the apartment across the hall with Chandler.

199 How many brothers and sisters did Joey have?
- A. Six
- B. Seven
- C. Eight

200 TOUGH ONE: What is the name of Joey's doctor?

201 Which of the following questions did Joey ask Ross while pretending to be Ross's unborn baby?
- A. "How come you don't live with Mommy?"
- B. "How come Mommy lives with that other lady?"
- C. "What's a lesbian?"
- D. All of the above

202 What two specific things did Joey do that caused his and Chandler's kitchen table to collapse?

A. He used the table to practice skateboarding for a movie role and then had sex on top of it.

B. He did a table dance on it for one of his dates and then threw his keys on it.

C. He had sex on the table and then threw his keys on it.

203 During a discussion about the sex of Ross's baby, what did the occasionally obtuse Joey say when Monica told Ross, "I'm sorry but I'm just excited about being an aunt"?

204 According to Joey, who could be a member of the Olympic Standing There Team?

A. Chandler, after Joey did all the work picking out a new kitchen table.

B. Ross, after Monica dominated a round of the table game Foosball and Ross did nothing.

C. Rachel, after watching Rachel sit and file her nails while everyone waited for their coffee orders.

205 TRUE OR FALSE: Joey and his family are Presbyterian.

206 What did Joey usually wear to sleep in?

A. Nothing

B. His underwear

C. His *Star Wars* pajamas

207 One of Joey's sister's husbands got a restraining order against *her*. Can you name this Tribbiani lass?

A. Gina

B. Tina

C. Marie

208 Joey was especially fond of a steakhouse called Tony's that had a terrific deal on their thirty-two-ounce steak. What was it?

    A. If you finished it, you got another one free.

    B. If you finished it, you got all the Caesar salad and steak fries you could eat.

    C. If you finished it, it was free.

209 What did Joey's girlfriend Melanie give him the day after he took Monica's romantic advice about being there "for her" and let her have all the fun in bed?

    A. Many, many fruit baskets

    B. A Stairmaster

    C. A car

210 According to Joey, what specific possession of Ross's was a "chick magnet"?

    A. His John Tesh CD collection

    B. His monkey Marcel

    C. His giant *Speed Racer* poster

211 According to Joey, what was the rule regarding food that could be served at a poker game?

    A. You could only serve food that could be eaten straight out of bag or box without benefit of kitchen appliances.

    B. You could only serve food that made you thirsty.

    C. You could only serve food with one syllable, like chips or dip or pretz.

212 FILL-IN-THE-BLANKS: During a cutthroat poker game, Joey folded using an amazingly descriptive metaphor. Fill in the missing words:

"I fold like a cheap _____
who got hit in the _____
by a _____ guy with _____
on his _____ ."

213 During a game of Pictionary, Joey couldn't get *Bye Bye Birdie* but did guess a movie's name by seeing nothing but a drawing of a kidney bean. What movie title did Joey successfully come up with?

214 What was the name of the single mother Joey helped during the delivery of her baby, and what was her favorite basketball team?

A. Lydia; the New York Knicks

B. Lydia; the Boston Celtics

C. Angela; the Chicago Bulls

215 What was Phoebe talking about when she told Joey that he would be making money "hand over fist"?

Part 3

The First Season

The Friends at Christmas (minus Joey!).

EPISODE 1
"The One Where Monica Gets a Roommate" [Pilot]

FRIEND FACTS: Let the bonding begin! This first episode of *Friends* introduced us to the Sensational Six and immediately dropped us into their various, interwoven lives. This episode had a different opening sequence in which the Friends all get in and actually *dance* in the fountain that is only seen in the later openings. (The song is still "I'll Be There For You" by the Rembrandts, though.) The story then begins in our favorite coffeehouse where we eavesdrop on what is obviously a continuing discussion of Monica Geller's dating life. We meet Chandler Bing and Joey Tribbiani, two roommates who share an apartment across from Monica's, and we are also introduced to the somewhat off-center Phoebe. Soon, Monica's brother Ross enters, consummately depressed because his wife has just left him for another woman, and then shortly thereafter, Rachel Green, Monica and Ross's high school friend, bursts in, still elaborately decked out in her *wedding dress*! Rachel has come to Monica for sanctuary after she left her fiancé Barry at the altar. And thus, the *Friends* saga begins. By the time this episode is over, Monica has been used; Rachel has moved in; Ross has put new furniture together; and Phoebe has told them all her incredibly strange life story.

FAVORITE MOMENTS: There are several delightful moments in this terrific episode. Rachel's attempted conciliatory phone conversation with her father is hilarious: People always told her she was a shoe, but what if she wanted to be a purse or a hat? "It's a metaphor, Daddy!" Phoebe trying to sing "My Favorite Things" to cheer Rachel up is classic Phebes.

Monica's spit take (with Paul the Wine Guy in the restaurant) is perfectly executed. And what is probably the most emotionally powerful moment occurs when Ross rhetorically asks Chandler and Joey whom could he ask out now that he's single, and we see a sad and lonely Rachel sitting in a window, as Jackson Browne sings, "If you ever need holding, call my name and I'll be there." Nice.

216 What was Chandler's response when Monica told him that she was not *dating* Paul the Wine Guy, that it was only two people going out to dinner and not having sex?

    A. "Did Paul the Wine Guy sign off on this itinerary or will you be surprising him with this terrific piece of news during the appetizers?"

    B. "Skip the dinner and subtract one person and you've just described every night of my own wretched life."

    C. "Sounds like a date to me."

217 What was Joey's answer to Ross's pain?

    A. "Strip joints!"

    B. "Hockey!"

    C. "The All-You-Can-Eat Special at Taco Bell!"

218 Rachel knew her pending marriage to Barry was a mistake when she realized she was more turned on by a certain *thing* than by Barry. Can you identify what persuaded Rachel to leave Barry waiting at the altar?

    A. A pair of sling back black pumps

    B. A Limoge gravy boat

    C. A diamond pendant

219 What toy did Barry remind Rachel of?

A. Mr. Potato Head
B. Malibu Ken
C. G. I. Joe

220 THINK ABOUT IT: Right after Rachel moved in with
Monica, the Friends all watched a soap opera during which
they chanted "Push her down the stairs!" to a certain character in the show. Even if the character had been able to
hear them, why wouldn't she have understood them?

221 As mentioned in the "Friends Facts" introduction,
Phoebe attempted to console Rachel by singing "My
Favorite Things" to her, only she didn't know the words.
Your mission is to provide Phoebe's last line, a lyric which
is quintessential Ms. Buffay.

Raindrops on roses

And whiskers on kittens

Doorbells and sleigh bells

And . . . thing with mittens

_____ _____, _____ _____ _____

222 Where were Rachel and Barry supposed to go for their
honeymoon?
A. France
B. Canada
C. Aruba

223 From the following list of "marital property," match
what Ross and Carol each got in their divorce settlement.
A. The furniture   1. Ross
B. The stereo   2. Carol
C. The good TV

D. Joey

E. Chandler

224 TRUE OR FALSE: Barry made love with his socks on.

225 Ross and Rachel split a cookie just before Ross inquired if he could ask her out sometime. What kind of cookie did they share?

A. A Fig Newton

B. An Oreo

C. A Pepperidge Farm Milano cookie

EPISODE 2
"The One With
the Sonogram at the End"

FRIEND FACTS: In this episode, a few of our Friends go through some rather traumatic—yet hilarious—experiences. Ross learns that his ex-wife Carol is pregnant with his baby and that she and Susan want him to be involved in the baby's life. Monica has her parents over for dinner and endures exquisite torture by her mother. Rachel decides to give Barry back his engagement ring but when she brings it to him at his office, she learns that he has begun a relationship with her almost maid of honor, Mindy. And finally, Ross accompanies Carol and Susan to the OB/GYN and sees a sonogram of his unborn child.

FAVORITE MOMENTS: My personal favorite moment in this episode (and one that got a *huge* laugh from the studio audience) is when Ross is showing the sonogram of his baby to the rest of them and Joey asks, "What are we supposed to be seeing here?" Chandler replies, "I don't know, but I think it's about to attack the Enterprise."

226 FILL-IN-THE-BLANK: During a discussion of how important kissing was to women, Chandler offered the brilliant insight of describing kissing as "pretty much like an opening act, you know? I mean, it's like the comedian you have to sit through before _____ _____ comes out."
  - A. Van Halen
  - B. Pink Floyd
  - C. Pearl Jam

227 According to Ross's assistant Marsha, why did the museum cavewoman look angry?
  - A. "She has issues."
  - B. "She has her period."
  - C. "She's prehistorically premenstrual."

228 What TV show were the Friends watching when Chandler remarked that he thought that this was the episode where "there was some kind of misunderstanding"?
  - A. *Gilligan's Island*
  - B. *Three's Company*
  - C. *The Brady Bunch*

229 Whom did Phoebe describe as "all chaotic and twirly"?
  - A. Joey
  - B. Rachel
  - C. Monica

230 In this episode, Ugly Naked Guy got a new piece of athletic equipment. What was it?

    A. A Stairmaster

    B. A Thighmaster

    C. Gravity boots

231 Rachel lost her engagement ring in an entrée. Can you name this dish?

    A. Lasagna

    B. Pasta Primavera

    C. Beef Wellington

232 Monica used a certain spice in her appetizers that her mother did not like. What was this condiment?

    A. Basil

    B. Curry

    C. Thyme

233 What did Monica make as a replacement dinner after her planned dish was ruined when the Friends had to dig through it for Rachel's lost engagement ring?

    A. Spaghetti.

    B. Hamburgers.

    C. She ordered in pizza.

234 TOUGH ONE: What was the name of Susan's OB/GYN?

235 Which of the following personal changes did Barry make after Rachel left him at the altar?

    A. He got a tan.

    B. He got hair plugs.

    C. He got contact lenses.

    D. He grew a beard.

EPISODE 3
"The One With The Thumb"

FRIEND FACTS: In this episode, Chandler goes back to smoking; Phoebe has trouble with her bank and then finds a human thumb in her can of soda; Ross learns the truth about a childhood pet; and Monica dates a guy named Alan whom all her Friends adore.

FAVORITE MOMENTS: One of my favorite moments and the scene which gets what is probably the biggest laugh in the episode is when Monica's new boyfriend Alan is introduced to the rest of the gang and says something that refers back to an earlier boyfriend of Monica's and which is absolutely hysterical. And to reveal any more than that would be to give away an answer from the Monica chapter—and that's not gonna happen, my friend!

236 According to Monica, the distance from the tip of a man's thumb to the tip of his index finger (when holding the fingers like a gun) was an indicator of a very important male measurement. What was it?
  A. The length of his erection.
  B. The length of his tongue.
  C. The length of his big toe.

237 TOUGH ONE: Rachel screwed up four orders in a row one day and Monica, Joey, Chandler, and Ross had to switch their beverages around in order to get what they really wanted. Match the beverage from the left column with the person who was supposed to get it from the right column:
  A. Joey's Decaf Cappuccino   1. Chandler
  B. Ross's Coffee Black   2. Ross

C. Chandler's Latté   3. Monica
D. Monica's Iced Tea   4. Joey

238 How much money did Phoebe's bank mistakenly credit her the first time her "Statement!" was wrong?
  A. $250
  B. $500
  C. $1,000

239 According to Phoebe, what would new shoes bought with the extra money the bank mistakenly gave her say every time she walked in them?

240 And according to Phoebe, what would those same shoes say every time she *skipped* in them?

241 What free appliance did Phoebe's bank give her (in addition to more free money) when she complained about the first mistake?
  A. A toaster
  B. A Mr. Coffee
  C. A football phone

242 FILL-IN-THE-BLANK: Complete Phoebe's fractured nursery rhyme:
  There was a crooked man
  Who had a crooked smile
  Who lived in a shoe

  _____

243 Monica's new boyfriend Alan did an impersonation of a member of the *Baywatch* cast. Who was it?

A. Susan Anton
B. David Hasselhoff
C. Yasmine Bleeth

244 Thanks to help from Alan, what team did Ross and Chandler's softball team slaughter?
A. The cast of *Cats*
B. A team of gas company employees
C. A team of Hasidic jewelers

245 Match the annoying habit from the left column with the offending Friend from the right column:

A. Cracks knuckles	1. Monica
B. Over-pronounces words	2. Rachel
C. Snorts when laughing	3. Ross
D. Chews hair	4. Chandler
E. Screws up orders	5. Phoebe
F. Smokes	6. Joey

EPISODE 4
"The One With George Stephanopoulos"

FRIEND FACTS: In this episode, Rachel gets her first paycheck as well as a depressing visit from three of her society girlfriends; Ross gets hit in the face with a puck on a very special anniversary and ends up at the emergency room; and Monica, Rachel, and Phoebe have a slumber party during which they reveal some deep secrets and end up with George Stephanopoulos's pizza.

FAVORITE MOMENTS: The scene in which the girls are watching George Stephanopoulos and his lady friend eat pizza is classic: Phoebe sees the woman go for a slice of pie and exclaims, "That's not for you, bitch!" (shocking the hell out of Rachel and Monica), after which a chagrined Phebes sheepishly covers her mouth with her hand. Also, the visit to the coffeehouse from Rachel's three squealing friends is absolutely hilarious.

246 At the beginning of this episode, the Friends ponder what they would each do if they were omnipotent for a day. Match the fantasy with the Friend:

A. World peace	1. Phoebe
B. Be omnipotent forever	2. Chandler
C. Bigger boobs	3. Ross
D. Good things for the rain forest	4. Joey
E. Commit suicide	5. Monica
F. No more hunger	6. Rachel

247 What disability did Phoebe's grandmother and her grandmother's new boyfriend have in common?

A. They were both blind.

B. They each used a walker.

C. They were both deaf.

248 FRIENDSPEAK DEPARTMENT: What did Joey reply when Ross sadly told him and Chandler that he didn't want to go to the hockey game with them and that all he wanted to do was go home and think about his ex-wife and her lesbian lover?

249 Rachel's three visiting society girlfriends all had major news for Rachel. Which of the following was NOT one of the important life events they told Rachel about?

A. One was engaged.

B. One just got her pilot's license.

C. One was pregnant.

D. One had just been made a partner in her daddy's firm.

250 With what liquor was Tiki Death Punch made?

A. Vodka

B. Rum

C. Tequila

251 Which two of the following games did Monica, Rachel, and Phoebe play at their slumber party?

A. Twister

B. Parcheesi

C. Operation

252 What credit card company called Rachel to inquire about the "unusual activity" on her card (which was actually the fact that she hadn't used the card in weeks)?

A. American Express

B. Diner's Club

C. Visa

253 Why, according to Phoebe's impeccable logic, was Rachel like Jack in "Jack and the Beanstalk"?

A. Because Jack lived in a village and Rachel lived in *the* Village.

B. Because "Jack" and "Rach" both had four letters.

C. Because Rachel had a really tall plant in her bedroom.

254 TRUE OR FALSE: The night of the slumber party, Monica, Rachel, and Phoebe ordered a pizza with mushrooms, green peppers, and onions.

255 While waiting on the apartment balcony for George Stephanopoulos to drop his towel, Monica, Rachel, and Phoebe each revealed a truth that they had up until then kept secret. Based on the secrets revealed, answer the following questions:

    A. Who revealed that she had slept   1, Rachel
         with Jason Hurley only a couple of
         hours after Monica had broken up
         with him?

    B. Who revealed that a Valentine Tommy   2. Monica
         Rollison had left for Monica was
         actually from Rachel?

    C. Who revealed that Rachel had peed   3. Phoebe
         in her pants in the seventh grade?

    D. Who revealed that a vegetarian
         paté that Phoebe had once eaten
         had actually had goose in it?

EPISODE 5
"The One With the East German Laundry Detergent"

FRIEND FACTS: In this episode, Monica and Joey go on a rather peculiar double date; Ross goes on a "laundry date" with Rachel during which they meet an absolutely *horrible* woman; Chandler breaks up with Janice and accidentally whacks her in the eye; and Phoebe decides she'd like a pink wardrobe.

FAVORITE MOMENTS: As Phoebe gravely explains to the others that Chandler just needed time to grieve after breaking up with Janice, Mr. Bing runs by the coffeehouse screaming, "I'm free! I'm free!" This is, for me, the funniest moment in this episode.

256 At the beginning of this episode, the Friends are all talking about what amazes them about the opposite sex. Match the amazement from the left column with the amazed from the right column:

A. That guys can pee standing up.	1. Phoebe
B. That guys can be mean and not even care.	2. Joey
C. That girls can see breasts anytime they want.	3. Rachel
D. Multiple orgasms!	4. Ross
E. That women can take off their bras through their sleeves.	

257 In what specific form of protest was Phoebe's boyfriend Tony involved when she broke up with him?

    A. He was chained to the front gate of a nuclear power plant.

    B. He was on a hunger strike.

    C. He was barricaded inside the office of the dean of students at his college.

258 FRIENDSPEAK DEPARTMENT: What did Joey's ex Angela say when Joey told her that she looked great?

    A. Yeah, I know. It's sort of like looking in a candy store window and not having any money, ain't it Joey?"

B. "Must be that Wonder Bra you bought me. Alan sends his thanks."

C. "That's 'cause I'm wearing a dress that accents my boobs."

259 In this episode, what kitchen task did the Friends watch Ugly Naked Guy do?

A. Lay kitchen tile

B. Clean the oven

C. Defrost the refrigerator

260 At what restaurant did Monica, Joey, Angela and Bob eat on their very strange "double date"?

A. Iridium

B. Fiorello's

C. The Russian Tea Room

261 What type of cartoon socks did Janice buy for Chandler?

A. Rocky (of "Rocky and Bullwinkle")

B. Beavis and Butthead

C. Bullwinkle (of "Rocky and Bullwinkle")

262 What was the name of the East German laundry detergent Ross brought to his "laundry date" with Rachel?

A. Das Soap

B. Weissvash

C. Überweiss

263 TRUE OR FALSE: One of the things that really annoyed Joey about Angela was the weird little nibbling noise she made when she ate.

264 What specific item of apparel did Rachel leave in with her whites that caused all of her laundry to turn pink?

    A. A red sock

    B. A pair of red panties

    C. A red T-shirt

265 When they were all out to dinner, Monica told Angela, Bob, and Joey a story about a cartoon character balloon that wouldn't inflate. What character was she talking about? (GIVEAWAY HINT: This character is actually mentioned in the title of a later episode of *Friends*.)

    A. Spider-Man

    B. Mickey Mouse

    C. Underdog

EPISODE 6
"The One With the Butt"

FRIEND FACTS: In this episode, Joey gets a job as a butt double and blows it; Chandler has a brief fling with a woman he meets at a terrible musical; Monica tries to prove she's not her mother and that she can be a kook; and Rachel rearranges the furniture.

FAVORITE MOMENTS: For me, the funniest moment in this episode occurs when Chandler walks in on Joey in the bathroom "preparing" for his new (butt) acting job and runs from the room screaming, "My eyes! My eyes!"

266 FOR *FRIENDS* TAPERS *ONLY*?: Joey performed the first musical number in *Freud!* This "song" was a little ditty that he sang to one of his female "patients." Can you fill in the missing words from the first verse of the song's lyrics:

All you want is a _____
What you envy's a _____
A ting through which you can _____
Or play vit or simply let hang

267 What didn't Phoebe like about the title of Joey's new musical, *Freud!*?

268 TOUGH ONE: What was the name of the talent agency that left Joey their card after his performance in *Freud!* (and which later got him the butt double job)?

    A. The Estelle Leonard Talent Agency

    B. StarWorks

    C. Book 'Em!

269 Which of the following guys were NOT involved with Aurora?

    A. Ross

    B. Rick

    C. Ethan

    D. Andrew

    E. Chandler

270 Joey was (almost) what big movie star's butt double?

    A. Dustin Hoffman

    B. Al Pacino

    C. Harvey Keitel

271 What movie featured a scene in which a lawyer shouted at a judge, "*You're* out of order!" (HINT: Joey performed a little of this scene when he learned he had been hired to play a certain movie star's butt double.)

A. *The Verdict*
B. *. . . And Justice for All*
C. *A Few Good Men*

272 What cosmetic did Joey borrow from Monica to rub on his butt?

A. Moisturizer
B. Concealer
C. Blush

273 Joey performed two takes in a shower as a butt double before he was fired. What did he do wrong in the first take?

A. He bounced his cheeks rhythmically.
B. He leaned to the left too much and made his crack uneven.
C. He clenched his butt cheeks.

274 What did Joey do wrong in his *second* take?

A. He tried to make his butt express "quiet desperation."
B. He tried to make his butt express "the joy of the water."
C. He spread when he had been told to squeeze.

275 To prove that she was not obsessive, Monica went to bed without putting something away. What did she (reluctantly) leave on her living room floor?

A. A pair of shoes
B. A towel
C. Her nylon jacket

EPISODE 7
"The One With the Blackout"

FRIEND FACTS: In this episode, New York is plunged into darkness during a widespread blackout; Chandler is trapped in a bank with übermodel Jill Goodacre and ends up needing to be Heimliched; Ross's decision to tell Rachel his true feelings about her proves futile when Rach meets and falls for an Italian stud named Paolo; and Joey fabricates a surprise birthday party for Monica.

FAVORITE MOMENTS: Unquestionably the funniest moment in this episode occurs in the scene when Paolo's cat leaps onto Ross's back out on the balcony and the dignified Mr. Geller runs about flailing and screaming as Monica, Phoebe, and Joey obliviously sing "Top of the World" in the living room.

276 Was Chandler stranded in a vestibule or an atrium?

277 How did Ugly Naked Guy hurt himself during the blackout?
   A. He stubbed his foot on the dining room table.
   B. He backed into the stove when the oven was on.
   C. He burned himself with some candles.

278 During the blackout, the Friends (except for the "incarcerated" Chandler, of course) all took turns revealing the strangest place they had ever had sex. Match the odd venue from the left column with the adventurous lover from the right column:
   A. Milwaukee   1. Monica
   B. Behind the "It's a Small World"   2. Ross
      exhibit at Disneyland

  C. On a pool table during senior year   3. Rachel
   of college
  D. At the foot of the bed   4. Joey
  E. In the women's room on the second   5. Phoebe
   floor of the New York Public Library

279 According to Joey, who was mayor of the Friend Zone?
  A. Chandler
  B. Ross
  C. Monica

280 FILL-IN-THE-LYRICS: Supply the missing words for this verse from Phoebe's scintillating "blackout" song:
  New York City has no power
  And the milk is getting _____
  But to me it is not scary
  'Cause I stay away from _____

281 What kind of antiseptic did Monica use on Ross after his back was shredded by Paolo's cat?
  A. Bactine
  B. Hydrogen peroxide
  C. Straight rubbing alcohol

282 FILL-IN-THE-BLANK: When Chandler decided that he *would* take a piece of gum from Jill Goodacre, he said to her, "On second thought, gum would be _____."

283 In an attempt to catnap Paolo's cat, the Weird Guy (whom we learn later on in the series is Mr. Heckles) said the cat was his and made up a phony name for the kitty. What was the name he came up with?

A. Buttons

B. Bob Buttons

C. Patty

284 What was the real name of Paolo's cat?

A. Tutti

B. Cara Mia

C. Bella

285 What amazingly descriptive term did Ross come up with to describe Paolo? (HINT: Think "crap!")

EPISODE 8
"The One Where Nana Dies Twice"

FRIEND FACTS: In this episode, Ross and Monica's Nana dies twice and at the cemetery Ross has his worst fear realized; Joey clandestinely watches a sporting event while Ross sleeps on Rachel's lap; Chandler is aghast to learn that people regularly think he's gay; Monica and her hypercritical mother come to a semi-understanding of each other; and Rachel looks at naked baby pictures of Ross.

FAVORITE MOMENTS: I have two favorite moments in "Nana Dies Twice," an episode that successfully swings from comedy to drama: The first is when Chandler, who has been trying to figure out why people have always thought he was gay, arrives at Monica's apartment for Nana's funeral and says, "Well, don't we look nice all dressed up?" After this is met with silence from the others, Chandler asks, "It's stuff like that, isn't it?" And my second favorite moment is at the end when Chandler asks his gay coworker Lowell if he has a "gay" quality about him that makes people think he's a homosexual. Lowell replies deadpan, "Speaking for my people, I would have to say no." (This reminded me of a scene in *Mad About You* when Paul asks a French waiter for "the fries of your people." Funny stuff.)

286 When did Chandler *first* learn that people always thought he was gay?
- A. In college when the master of the only gay fraternity on campus tried to recruit him for the frat.
- B. When Lowell from financial services slipped him a note with a condom inside it.
- C. When his female coworker Shelly tried to fix him up on a date with a guy.

287 When Rachel first met Chandler, she, too, thought he was gay. What changed her mind?
- A. Rachel ran into Chandler when he was out on a date with Janice.
- B. Chandler spent Phoebe's entire birthday party talking to Rachel's breasts.
- C. Rachel saw a girl dressed in only a T-shirt come out of his bedroom when she went across the hall one morning to borrow some coffee.

288 What type of coffee sweetener did Nana steal?
- A. Sweet & Low packets
- B. Equal packets
- C. Sugar packets

289 Phoebe's friend Debbie was struck by lightning on a miniature golf course. According to Phebes, what inanimate object was Debbie reincarnated as?

A. A yellow Post-It note

B. A yellow pencil

C. A banana

290 How did Ross and Monica's dad Jack want to be buried?

A. He wanted to be interred in a mausoleum.

B. He wanted to be buried at sea.

C. He wanted to be cremated and have his ashes spread at Churchill Downs.

291 TRUE OR FALSE: Even though Chandler was sure he could "get a Brian" *if* he was gay and *if* he wanted to, the general consensus was that Brian was *way* out of Chandler's league.

292 According to her mother, which of Monica's body parts were not her "best feature"?

A. Her breasts

B. Her feet

C. Her ears

293 What specific sporting event did Joey watch on a tiny TV in his coat at Nana's funeral?

A. A hockey game

B. A football game

C. A basketball game

294 How many muscle relaxants did Ross take at Nana's funeral reception after Phoebe determined his back was in spasm?

A. two

B. four

C. six

295 THE "WHAT GOES AROUND, COMES AROUND" DEPARTMENT: What was the name of the coffeehouse where Nana and her friends hung out when they were young?

    A. Central Perk

    B. Daily Grind

    C. Java Joe's

EPISODE 9
"The One Where Underdog Gets Away"

FRIEND FACTS: Monica decides to make Thanksgiving dinner for everyone; Joey becomes a free clinic "disease poster boy"; Ross talks (and sings) to his unborn child through Carol's belly; and Underdog gets away.

FAVORITE MOMENTS: Ross impulsively slaps away Susan's hand as he sings *"The Monkees* Theme Song" to his unborn child through Carol's belly. Susan laughs and goodnaturedly whacks him on the head. A nice bonding moment between an ex-husband and his wife's new lesbian lover.

296 Why couldn't Monica and Ross eat Thanksgiving with their parents?

    A. Their parents decided to go out to dinner alone for Thanksgiving.

    B. Their parents decided to go to Puerto Rico for Thanksgiving.

    C. Monica and Ross couldn't afford the plane fare for the trip home.

Monica makes a point to Rachel. (Jennifer Aniston, left,
Courteney Cox, right)

297 FILL-IN-THE-BLANK: Phoebe and her grandmother celebrated Thanksgiving at Christmas because Grandma's new boyfriend was _____.

    A. "nocturnal"

    B. "a Capricorn"

    C. "lunar"

298 Ross found out that Susan talked to his unborn child through Carol's stomach during a visit to the two women's apartment. Why did Ross go there in the first place?

    A. To pick up a skull he lent to Carol.

    B. To drop off Marcel for "monkeysitting."

    C. To pick up the rent.

299 What was Susan talking about when she told Ross, "Well, you know, you have to take a course. Otherwise they don't let you do it"?

300 Who is BoBo the Sperm Guy?

    A. Chandler

    B. Ross

    C. Fun Bobby

301 Which of the Friends selected a Thanksgiving menu of tomato soup, grilled cheese sandwiches, and a family size bag of Funyuns? (HINT: He boycotted all Pilgrim holidays.)

    A. Chandler

    B. Joey

    C. Ross

302 What was Joey's "disease poster boy" name?

303 Fill in the missing words from Ross's special rendition of "*The Monkees* Theme Song":

Hey, hey, you're my baby,

And I can't wait to meet you,

When you come out I'll buy you a _____,

And then we'll go to the _____.

Hey, hey, I'm your daddy,

I'm the one without any _____.

304 Who is "Smirky"?

A. Chandler

B. Joey

C. Ross

305 Joey ripped off the bottom of his "disease" poster until he came to a caption he liked. What did he finally accept?

A. "Bladder Control Problems"

B. "Hemorrhoids"

C. "Winner of Three Tony Awards"

EPISODE 10
"The One With the Monkey"

FRIEND FACTS: In this New Year's Eve episode, Ross adopts Marcel the monkey and introduces him to his friends; Phoebe begins—and ends—a relationship with David the Scientist Guy; Joey dates a single mom; and the Friends make a New Year's Eve pact that starts with them all agreeing to have dinner as a group, but which ends up turning into a huge party, at which none of them has anyone to kiss.

FAVORITE MOMENTS: My absolute favorite scene—the one that had me laughing hysterically—really consists of nothing more than one word. But what a word! This moment occurs at the disastrous New Year's Eve party at Monica and Rachel's apartment when physicist Max, David's colleague and fellow grant recipient, greets Phoebe and David. David has already told Max that he will not be going to Minsk with him because he doesn't want to break up with Phoebe. Max is understandably distraught and when he approaches David and Phebes, he greets her by nodding and saying, "Yoko." (And please, tell me you all *do* get this gag, don't you?)

306 What, according to Ross, does the word "pathet" mean?

    A. It's Sanskrit for "really cool way to live."

    B. It's Esperanto for "lesbian life partner."

    C. It's Yiddish for "Many thanks in your belly button."

307 COMPLETE THE LYRICS: Fill in the missing words from this original Phoebe Buffay composition:

    I made a man with eyes of coal

    And a smile so bewitchin'

    How was I supposed to know

    That my mom was _____

308 Who are The Noisy Boys?

309 David the Scientist Guy thought Phoebe was the most beautiful woman he'd ever seen, but his pal Max preferred a certain blonde actress. Whom did Max like better?

    A. Melanie Griffith

    B. Daryl Hannah

    C. Meg Ryan

310 Phoebe told the gang said that David the Scientist reminded her of a guy with whom she saw a certain movie. Name this flick.

    A. *An Officer and a Gentleman*

    B. *Sleepless in Seattle*

    C. *Four Weddings and a Funeral*

311 What specific cooking utensils did Marcel play with in Monica's kitchen?

    A. Her frying pans

    B. Her basters

    C. Her spatulas

312 Why was Fun Bobby not so much fun at the New Year's Eve party?

    A. His moped had just been stolen.

    B. His grandfather had just died.

    C. He had just gotten mugged.

313 TRUE OR FALSE: Marcel could juggle balled-up socks and a melon at the same time.

314 Janice planned on writing something ("in glitter") on the new picture of her and Chandler that Ross took. What was she planning on writing?

    A. "Reunited"

    B. "Jan & Chan 4-Ever"

    C. "Team Bing"

315 Who finally caved and kissed Chandler after he repeatedly shrieked "Somebody kiss me!" after the ball dropped?

EPISODE 11
"The One With Mrs. Bing"

FRIEND FACTS: In this episode, Monica and Phoebe inadvertently put a guy into a coma and end up becoming obsessed with him; Chandler's mother Nora, a famous romance novelist, comes to town and winds up in an embarrassing situation with Ross; Joey defends his mother's sex appeal; Ross and Chandler feud; and Rachel begins writing a sexy, wildly misspelled romance novel.

FAVORITE MOMENTS: I have two favorite moments in this episode: One is the scene in which Nora Bing reveals on national TV that she bought Chandler his first condoms; and the other is when Ross makes funny use of a shot glass at a Mexican restaurant. In the condom scene, everyone turns and looks at Chandler after his mother's humiliating revelation and he adds, "And then, he burst into flames." And in the Mexican restaurant, a drunken Ross puts the shot glass in his eye and asks if anyone wants him to appraise anything. (I used to be a jeweler so maybe I find this funnier than the average rabbit?)

316 In the incident in which Coma Guy becomes Coma Guy, Phoebe and Monica are at a newsstand looking for the previous day's *Daily News*. Why did Phebes want yesterday's paper?

    A. She wanted to check the weather forecast and see if it was right.

    B. She wanted to check her horoscope and see if it was right.

    C. She liked to read news that she already knew.

317 According to Phoebe, what did dents in a guy's knuckles indicate about him?

    A. It meant that he was a sexual dynamo.

    B. It meant that he was a sensitive nurturer.

    C. It meant that he was artistic.

318 Which of the following titles is NOT one of Nora Tyler Bing's romance novels?

    A. *Euphoria Unbound*

    B. *Mistress Bitch*

    C. *Euphoria at Midnight*

    D. *A Woman Undone*

319 For what Chinese dish did Nora Bing get a craving after having sex?

    A. General Cho's Chicken

    B. Kung Po Chicken

    C. Shrimp Lo Mein

320 Phoebe and Monica were diligent about taking care of Coma Guy while he was in the hospital. Match the good deed from the left column with the caregiver from the right column:

    A. She read the paper to him.   1. Monica

    B. She knit him a sweater.   2. Phoebe

    C. She shaved him.

    D. She changed his pajamas.

    E. She played the guitar and sang to him.

    F. She gave him an Etch-A-Sketch.

    G. She gave him a foot massager.

321 What specific alcoholic beverage did the Friends, Nora, and Paolo do shots of at the Mexican Village Restaurant?

    A. Vodka

    B. Sambucco

    C. Tequila

322 Which of the following was Nora Bing's "formula" for her romance novels?

    A. two scenes of oral sex, one steamy cab ride, and three foreign capitals.

    B. six European cities and thirty euphemisms for male genitalia.

    C. two corrupt politicians, a male stripper, and twenty euphemisms for breasts.

323 Who told Ross that his kissing Chandler's mom was no big deal—"in Bizarro World!"?

    A. Joey

    B. Rachel

    C. Monica

324 Who called Ross "Motherkisser"?

    A. Chandler

    B. Joey

    C. Monica

325 Can a love stick be liberated from its denim prison?

EPISODE 12
"The One With
the Dozen Lasagnas"

FRIEND FACTS: In this episode, Monica tries to get rid of twelve unwanted lasagnas; Ross learns the sex of his baby; Rachel and Paolo split up; Chandler and Joey go in on a new kitchen table; and Rachel learns three important things about Phoebe.

FAVORITE MOMENTS: Monica's "You suck!" to Chandler during a heated game of Foosball is hilarious, and Ross mistaking Carol's friend Tanya for, ahem, someone else slayed me (and the studio audience, for that matter! This scene got a *huge* laugh).

326 At the beginning of this episode, the Friends all hum the theme to a popular TV sitcom, after which Ross attempts to start another TV theme "hum-along." What two show themes were "performed"?

    A. *Bewitched* and *The Andy Griffith Show*

    B. *The Brady Bunch* and *The Addams Family*

    C. *The Odd Couple* and *I Dream of Jeannie*

327 For what rock star did Ross mistake Carol and Susan's friend Tanya?

    A. Huey Lewis

    B. Bruce Springsteen

    C. Rod Stewart

328 TRUE OR FALSE: As soon as Carol told him that *she* knew, Ross wanted to be told the sex of his baby.

329 Who is Angela Delvecchio?

    A. Carol's OB/GYN.

    B. Chandler's roommate before Joey.

    C. A girl Joey had sex with on his and Chandler's kitchen table.

330 Where did Paolo make a pass at Phoebe?

    A. At the massage parlor where Phoebe worked.

    B. In Monica's apartment.

    C. In the coffeehouse when Rachel was busy.

331 TRUE OR FALSE: Joey suggested buying patio furniture for their kitchen.

332 Phoebe told Rachel three things that she should know about her. Fill in the third "thing": "I make the best _____ cookies in the world."

    A. "oatmeal-raisin"

    B. "chocolate chip"

    C. "lemon"

333 Who is Pigman?

    A. Ross

    B. Joey

    C. Paolo

334 Who is the "Anti-Paolo"?

335 Who (rather appropriately, if you think about it) inadvertently revealed to Ross that he was having a son?

    A. Rachel

    B. Monica

    C. Phoebe

EPISODE 13
"The One With the Boobies"

FRIEND FACTS: In this episode, Chandler sees Rachel's boobies and the "Booby Payback Express" begins; Phoebe dates a psychiatrist named Roger who psychoanalyzes all the others and incurs their loathing; Joey finds out that his dad has been seeing another woman for years; and Joey and Chandler sleep together.

FAVORITE MOMENTS: My favorite moment in this episode is Roger the psychiatrist's impassioned "slash and burn" analysis of the Friends and their coffeehouse time spent together after Phoebe reveals to him that the others had a "liking problem" with him. He used words like "dysfunctional," "emotionally stunted," "codependent," and said the cups they drank out of "might as well have nipples on them." Very funny scene.

336 FILL-IN-THE-BLANK: When Rachel covered herself up with a quilt after Chandler saw her boobies, he said, "That's a relatively open weave and I can still see your _____ area."

337 Who is Sparky?

338 Which of the following positions did Joey Sr.'s mistress Ronnie, the pet mortician, say were the two most popular for stuffing dead pets?
    A. Chasing their tail
    B. Jumping to catch a Frisbee
    C. Sitting up and begging

339 How long had Joey Sr. been seeing Ronnie when Joey found out about her?

    A. one year

    B. three years

    C. six years

340 What group of toys did Roger determine had a lot to do with Rachel's screwed-up mental state?

    A. The Barbie and Ken collection

    B. The Weebles collection

    C. The Potato Head family

341 Into what position did Chandler say he'd liked to be placed if he was stuffed after he died?

    A. Eating a piece of pizza

    B. Waving goodbye

    C. Looking for his keys

342 Who is Kicky?

343 TRUE OR FALSE: Rachel saw Joey's pee-pee.

344 What rock star did Joey's mother say her husband would look like in an ideal world?

    A. Rod Stewart

    B. Elvis

    C. Sting

345 TRUE OR FALSE: Joey saw Monica's boobies.

EPISODE 14
"The One With the Candy Hearts"

FRIEND FACTS: In this Valentine's Day episode, Chandler goes on a blind date with the amazingly shrill Janice; Monica, Rachel, and Phoebe perform a "cleansing" boyfriend bonfire ritual that ends up requiring firefighters; and Ross goes on his first date in years and finds himself at the same table as his ex-wife and her new "companion."

FAVORITE MOMENTS: Without a doubt, the boyfriend bonfire: An absolute classic TV moment.

346 As part of Phoebe's "cleansing ritual," Monica and Rachel were given two choices, one of which was burning all the stuff their ex-boyfriends gave them. What was the other option?

    A. Reciting ancient Celtic curses while bathing in sacramental oil.

    B. Chanting and dance around naked with sticks.

    C. Cutting off all their hair and burying it.

347 On his blind date with Joey and Lorraine, who was Chandler's date?

    A. Janice

    B. Monica

    C. Rachel

348 Joey's date was able to do something unique with her toes. What was it?

    A. She could dial a phone.

    B. She could pull down a zipper.

    C. She could pick up quarters.

349 What was Janice talking about when she told Chandler, "You can make puppets out of them and use them in your Theater of Cruelty!"?

    A. All the "Chandler heads" she had cut out of all her photos.

    B. The eleven pairs of white athletic socks Chandler left at her apartment after he broke up with her.

    C. The colored condom collection Chandler left at her apartment after he broke up with her.

350 What specific take-out dessert item did Joey's date order to take home and "slather" his body with?

    A. Tapioca pudding

    B. Chocolate mousse

    C. Cherry cheesecake

351 For the boyfriend bonfire, what did the girls use *instead of* the required sage branches and sacramental wine?

    A. A leftover Caesar salad and a half bottle of Zima

    B. A Popsicle stick and some Gatorade

    C. Oregano and Fresca

352 What was Rachel talking about when she told Phoebe, "If we had that, we wouldn't be doing the ritual in the first place"?

353 What was the item of boyfriend debris that started the fire in Monica and Rachel's apartment?

    A. Paul the Wine Guy's Iridium stick matches

    B. The last of Paolo's Grappa

    C. Nokalooloo's Bic lighter

354 How many fireman guys responded to the girls' boyfriend bonfire?

355 How did Ross end up alone with his ex-wife Carol at the Japanese restaurant?

   A. Susan got beeped and Kristen got fed-up with Ross ignoring her.
   B. Susan never showed and Kristen left with an old boyfriend.
   C. Susan and Kristen left together . . . if you know what I mean.

EPISODE 15
"The One With the Stoned Guy"

FRIEND FACTS: In this episode, Chandler gets promoted, quits his job, and then learns that what he was doing was exactly what he is suited for; Monica "auditions" for a job as head chef for a restaurant owner who is not exactly in the best condition to appreciate her culinary skills; Ross dates a young lady who wants him to talk dirty to her, a skill Joey is happy to teach him; and Rachel reluctantly agrees to work temporarily for Monica.

FAVORITE MOMENTS: Without a doubt, the funniest sequence in this episode is the entire "dinner audition" scene in Monica's apartment, during which a wasted Steve the Restaurant Guy (played hilariously by a snide Jon Lovitz) wreaks havoc and transforms Monica's carefully planned "tasting" menu into an "eat everything (and anything!) in sight" stoned binge.

356 Who is Mr. Suity Man?

   A. Ross

B. Chandler

C. Joey

357 TOUGH ONE: Where was Steve's new restaurant located?

A. Tenth Street

B. Fifth Avenue

C. Avenue of the Americas

358 What, precisely, was Phoebe's role during Monica's "dinner audition"?

A. To make yummy noises

B. To laugh at Steve's jokes

C. To make ice

359 Which of the following tests did Chandler take as part of his career counseling program?

A. Aptitude

B. Intelligence

C. Personality

D. All of the above

360 What did Chandler say he once did during the Olympics in Innsbruck in '76?

A. He said he ran the 100 meter and came in fifth.

B. He said he got stoned with Linda Ronstadt— "although she'll never admit it now."

C. He said he waited tables.

361 What "dirty word" did Ross say to Celia when she prodded him to say something hot to her?

A. "booby"

B. "vulva"

C. "pee-pee"

Steve the obnoxious Restaurant Guy and Monica in a scene from the episode, "The One With the Stoned Guy," with guest star Jon Lovitz.

362 Who walked in on Ross and Joey as Joey was demonstrating to Ross how to talk dirty during sex?

    A. Monica

    B. Chandler

    C. Phoebe

363 Who is Greeter Girl?

364 TOUGH ONE: What, precisely, did Steve the Restaurant Guy say when Monica told him that she had prepared him an appetizer of rock shrimp ravioli in a cilantro ponzo sauce with just a touch of minced ginger? (HINT: His inspired exclamation included the words "ass" and "Judy" in the same sentence!)

365 Which of the following edibles did stoned Steve want to eat during Monica's audition?

    A. Taco shells

    B. Sugar-Os

    C. Macaroni and cheese

    D. Gummy Bears

    E. All of the above

EPISODE 16
"The One With Two Parts" Part 1

FRIEND FACTS: In this first episode of a two-part story, we meet Phoebe's twin sister Ursula (who Joey immediately begins hitting on); Marcel the monkey makes some adjustments to Ross's answering machine and TV; Chandler starts dating an attractive employee instead of firing her; and Ross attends Lamaze class with Carol and Susan.

FAVORITE MOMENTS: There are two in this episode: The appearance of *Mad About You*'s Jamie Buchman and Fran Devanow at Central Perk (a terrific TV moment) is one. And the other (one of my favorite bits) occurs at Lamaze class when Ross pretends a doll is a football and tells Susan to "Go deep."

366 TRUE OR FALSE: Marcel the monkey knew how to erase the messages from Ross's answering machine.

367 After Joey ran into Ursula at Riff's, he asked Phoebe to guess who he saw. Which of the following people did Phoebe guess? (HINT: She guessed three people before giving up.)

    A. Morley Safer

    B. Tom Hanks

    C. Sting

    D. Bette Midler

    E. The Woman Who Cuts Her Hair

    F. Liam Neeson

368 Marcel changed Ross's TV so that it broadcast a Spanish soundtrack instead of English. Which of the following shows did the Friends watch in Spanish?

    A. *Family Matters*

    B. *Laverne and Shirley*

    C. *The Waltons*

    D. *The Patty Duke Show*

    E. All of the above

369 Who was assigned the job of taking the Christmas lights down off Monica and Rachel's apartment balcony, Monica or Rachel?

370 When Joey visited Riff's, he ordered coffee. What did Ursula bring him instead?

    A. Turkey burger appetizers and an iced tea.

    B. A tuna melt and four plates of curly fries.

    C. A whole barbecued chicken.

371 What does A.N.U.S. stand for?

A. Annual Net Usage Statistics

B. Accrued Net Unemployment Status

C. Aggregate Normal Utilization Stage

372 TRUE OR FALSE: Mr. Heckles had cats.

373 What entertainment spectacle did Joey take Ursula to see on their first date?

A. The Big Apple Circus

B. Carly Simon Live in Grand Central Station

C. The Ice Capades

374 How did Chandler get out of firing Nina Bookbinder?

A. He told his boss she was crazy and suicidal.

B. He hid in his office bathroom every time his boss came looking for him.

C. He told his boss she was holding his A.N.U.S. hostage and that the company would collapse if she were fired.

375 How did Rachel get hurt and end up at the emergency room at the beginning of Part 2 of this story?

A. She fell asleep under her tanning lamp.

B. She hung herself by the ankle with the Christmas lights electrical cord and fell off the balcony.

C. She threw her back out during a rather spirited game of Twister.

EPISODE 17
"The One With Two Parts" Part 2

FRIEND FACTS: In this conclusion to a terrific two-part story, Monica and Rachel switch identities at the emergency room and end up dating two hot doctors who don't know their real names; Joey attempts to continue his relationship with Phoebe's sister Ursula; Marcel the monkey winds up in the hospital, forcing Ross to confront his pending fatherhood; and *Friends* gets dubbed into Spanish.

FAVORITE MOMENTS: The hilarious scene in Monica's living room where Rachel and Monica tear each other apart in front of the two studly *ER* doctors who don't know they've switched identities is my favorite in this second half.

376 A BRIEF MUSICAL INTERLUDE: The song, "What's the Frequency, Kenneth?" was played at the party for Phoebe in Monica's apartment. Who performs this song?

> A. REM
> B. U2
> C. INXS

377 Who brought the birthday cake to Phoebe's surprise party?

> A. Chandler
> B. Joey
> C. Ross

378 When the ER doctors visited Monica and Rachel, they brought wine from a rather obscure vineyard. Can you name this winery?

   A. Chateau de Newark
   B. The cellars of Ernest and Tovah Borgnine
   C. Vintage of Fabio

379 One of the ER docs tried to convince the other medico that Monica and Rachel were normal by citing two facts about the girls and the apartment. What were they?

   A. There were Milk Duds in a bowl on the coffee table and "It's fact: All Milk Duds eaters are ipso facto normal."
   B. Neither of them wore blue eye shadow.
   C. There were no pagan altars or piles of bones in the corners.

380 During their date with the docs, Monica and Rachel (pretending to be Rachel and Monica of course) tore each other apart to score points with the doctors. Match the following insults with the person to whom it was assigned:

   A. Selfish   1. Monica
   B. Bossy   2. Rachel
   C. Spoiled   3. Both of them
   D. Fat in high school
   E. Wet the bed
   F. Used her breasts to get attention
   G. Slept with Billy Dresden on her parents' bed

381 What did Phoebe give Ursula for her birthday?

   A. A gift certificate for an aura cleansing
   B. A Judy Jetson Thermos
   C. An E-Z Bake Oven

382 What did Ursula give Phoebe for her birthday?

    A. The sweater Joey gave her

    B. A Judy Jetson Thermos

    C. An E-Z Bake Oven

383 During the Scrabble game in which Marcel choked, how many points did the word "kidney" score?

384 TOUGH ONE: What Scrabble letters did Marcel swallow and what did Chandler theorize he was trying to spell?

385 What sporting activity did the Friends watch Ugly Naked Guy do as they all conversed in Spanish?

    A. The ThighMaster

    B. The Hula Hoop

    C. The Stairmaster

EPISODE 18
"The One With All the Poker"

FRIEND FACTS: In this episode, Ross, Chandler, and Joey reluctantly agree to allow Monica, Phoebe, and Rachel into their sacrosanct poker game, except that they first have to teach the ladies how to play poker; Rachel lands an interview for a job she really, really wants; and Ross and Marcel "have words" over the Capuchin monkey's playing of a certain CD.

FAVORITE MOMENTS: My favorite scene in this episode is when an *exceptionally* cute Rachel sings her "I have got your money" song to Ross after she beats him in poker.

386 What song did the Friends whistle in unison as they stuffed Rachel's résumés into envelopes?

    A. The *Odd Couple* theme
    B. The *Bewitched* theme
    C. The *Bridge on the River Kwai* theme

387 During one of the guys' poker games, how did Joey mistake a "3" for an "8"?

    A. He made the mistake because there was a piece of chocolate on the card.
    B. He made the mistake because "I was holding it upside down."
    C. He made the mistake because "I thought we were playing pinochle."

388 TRUE OR FALSE: Dee was the sarcastic sister on *What's Happening!*

389 What "snacks" did Monica make for the Friends' first co-ed poker game?

    A. Basil rice pilaf and chocolate mousse
    B. Salmon roulettes and assorted crudités
    C. Rock shrimp ravioli and spinach salad

390 During one of the poker games, Phoebe threw away two Jacks. What was her reason for this discard?

    A. She didn't like the way one of them was looking at her.
    B. They both reminded her of an albino she once knew who used to wash windows at the Port Authority.
    C. Neither of them looked happy.

391 What CD did Marcel put on and dance to in Ross's apartment?

    A. *The Lion King*

    B. "Muskrat Love"

    C. "The Lion Sleeps Tonight"

392 What game were the Friends playing when Monica "accidentally" threw a dish across the room?

    A. Pictionary

    B. Monopoly

    C. Trivial Pursuit

393 When Rachel got called in for a job interview at a major department store, Phoebe told her, "It's like the mother ship is calling you home." What store was Phoebe talking about?

    A. Bloomingdales

    B. Saks Fifth Avenue

    C. Filene's

394 When Aunt Iris came over to teach the girls how to play poker, she "bluffed" that she had hit a certain TV star with her car on the way to the apartment. Who did she say she ran over?

    A. Bob Barker

    B. Tony Randall

    C. Don Knotts

395 FILL-IN-THE-MISSING-LYRICS: Rachel made up a song for Ross and sang it to him after she won a big hand of poker. Fill in the missing lyrics of Rachel's "composition":

"Well, I have got your money
And you'll never _____ it
And your _____ still open
Ha, I made you _____"

EPISODE 19
"The One Where
the Monkey Gets Away"

FRIEND FACTS: In this episode, Rachel finds out that her ex-fiancé Barry is getting married; she "monkey-sits" Marcel and promptly loses him; Ross decides to pursue a relationship with Rachel; Monica and Rachel meet an old high school "friend"; Phoebe gets shot in the butt; and the Friends browse through Monica's high school yearbook.

FAVORITE MOMENTS: Phoebe's slow-motion dive through the air as she protectively shields Marcel from a rendezvous with a tranquilizer dart as the theme from *Shaft* plays on the soundtrack is a classic *Friends* moment!

396 How did Rachel find out that her ex-fiancé Barry was marrying her almost maid of honor, Mindy?

- A. She read their engagement notice in the country club newsletter that her mother sent her.
- B. Mindy cattily told her when she "accidentally" speed-dialed Rachel's number by mistake.
- C. Barry nonchalantly mentioned it as he was cleaning her teeth.

397 FILL-IN-THE-BLANK: When Marcel the monkey correctly brought Ross a container of rice, he remarked to Rachel,

"He's finally mastered the difference between 'Bring me the' and '_____.' "

398 According to Ross, Rachel went on a certain type of "Embargo" after her breakup with Barry. What was it?

    A. A Semen Embargo

    B. A Testosterone Embargo

    C. A Penis Embargo

399 In this episode, Joey and Chandler saw a Hugh Grant movie (*Four Weddings and a Funeral*, perhaps?) that neither of them liked. Match the following "reviews" with the correct Friend.

    A. Joey   1. "Total chick flick"

    B. Chandler   2. "Suckfest"

400 When Ross decided to pursue a relationship with Rachel, he described his intentions by using a word that Chandler said was like something from the 1890s. What "antique" word did Ross use?

    A. He said he wanted to "court" her.

    B. He said he wanted to "romance" her.

    C. He said he wanted to "woo" her.

401 What were Rachel and Marcel watching when Marcel pooped in Aunt Monica's shoe?

    A. *The Lion King*

    B. A soap opera

    C. A *National Geographic* special about the rain forest

402 What color was the shoe of Monica's that Marcel pooped in?

A. Black

B. Red

C. Brown

403 After Marcel escaped the apartment, Chandler mused that since it was the primate's first time in New York, he'd probably do some "touristy" things. What activities did Chandler speculate Marcel might try?

A. Go see *The Phantom of the Opera* and eat at Elaine's.

B. Go see *Cats* and eat at the Russian Tea Room.

C. Visit the Statue of Liberty and eat in Chinatown.

404 What type of food did Mr. Heckles leave in the hall outside his apartment?

A. A piece of cheesecake

B. Some borscht

C. A Belgian waffle

405 Who was Patty?

EPISODE 20
"The One With
the Evil Orthodontist"

FRIEND FACTS: In this episode, Chandler (sort of) falls for Danielle, a girl he dated once; Rachel has a fling with her ex-fiancé Barry while Barry's *new* fiancé asks Rachel to be her maid of honor; and the Friends make contact with a neighbor with a telescope.

FAVORITE MOMENTS: I like the scene in which a "ready-for-a-fight" Joey calls the nosy neighbor with the telescope and ends up melting under the weight of an onslaught of compliments about his physique.

406 TRUE OR FALSE: Chandler would rather be Mr. Peanut than Mr. Salty.

407 In this episode, Ugly Naked Guy got a new piece of athletic equipment. What was it?
  A. A Stairmaster
  B. A Thighmaster
  C. Gravity boots

408 Complete Chandler's remark when Phoebe told him and Joey to "stop being so testeroney": He replied, "Which by the way, is the *real* _____ treat."

409 Name the New York restaurant where Barry and Rachel had lunch the day they had sex on Barry's dentist chair.
  A. The Rainbow Room
  B. The Four Seasons
  C. The Russian Tea Room

410 What perfume did Barry buy for Rachel the day they had sex on Barry's dentist chair?
  A. Chanel
  B. Passion
  C. Wings

411 What was the name of Barry's new fiancé (the woman who was also almost Rachel's maid of honor)?

412 What dental hygiene product did Monica find in Rachel's hair after her "dentist chair" date with Barry?

    A. Plaque rinse

    B. Dental floss

    C. Toothpaste

413 What did Chandler exclaim when Ross absentmindedly said, "Four letters, circle or hoop"?

414 TRUE OR FALSE: Sydney Marx, the neighbor with the telescope, was really a woman.

415 What actress did Sydney Marx tell Monica she looked like when she wore her green dress?

    A. Demi Moore

    B. Susan Lucci

    C. Ingrid Bergman

EPISODE 21
"The One With Fake Monica"

FRIEND FACTS: In this episode, a rambunctious and confident woman who becomes known as "Fake Monica" takes on Monica's identity and goes on a spending spree with her charge card; Joey tries to find the perfect stage name (with some not-so-helpful help from Chandler); and Marcel reaches sexual maturity, necessitating that Ross (gasp!) give him up.

FAVORITE MOMENTS: I like the scene in which Monica comes home drunk after an afternoon with Fake Monica, sticks her head under the faucet for a drink, and exclaims "Water rules!" when she comes up for air.

416 Which of the following things did Fake Monica do with Monica's charge card?

    A. She spent $300 on art supplies.

    B. She went horseback riding in the park.

    C. She took classes at the New School.

    D. All of the above

417 Upon reaching sexual maturity, which of Rachel's dolls did Marcel decide to hump?

    A. Raggedy Ann

    B. Raggedy Andy

    C. Curious George

418 Chandler suggested three "stage names" for Joey. Which one of the three did Joey actually use?

    A. Joey Peponi

    B. Joey Switzerland

    C. Joseph Stalin

419 TOO EASY?: Who was Fake Monica talking about when she showed up at tap class and asked, "Who's the new tense girl?"

420 What was Ross's first choice for a zoo for Marcel?

    A. The San Diego Zoo

    B. The Miami Zoo

    C. The Scranton Zoo

421 What is the punchline to the "Popes in a Volkswagen" joke?

422 Manana and Fake Monica went on an open call to what Broadway musical?

    A. *Grease*

    B. *Miss Saigon*

    C. *Cats*

423 TRUE OR FALSE: Fake Monica ended up at Rikers Island.

424 What did Phoebe give "Little Monkey Guy" Marcel as a going-away present?

    A. A poem

    B. A box of Pampers

    C. A bag of pistachios

425 What salacious stage name did the obtuse Joey use when he read for the role of Mercutio?

    A. I. P. Daly

    B. Holden McGroin

    C. Chuck U. Farley

EPISODE 22
"The One With the Ick Factor"

FRIEND FACTS: In this episode, Rachel starts having sex dreams involving all the guys—except Ross; Ross carries a beeper for when Carol goes into labor, but he keeps getting calls for a male outcall service; Monica does something "icky" that is also a felony in forty-eight states; and Phoebe goes to work for Chandler.

FAVORITE MOMENTS: I love the scenes when everyone imitates Chandler's stylized way of speaking: "Could that report BE

any later?"; "The hills are alive with the sound OF music";
"That is so NOT true." Very funny stuff.

426 What was the name of Phoebe's "at home" workshop
that ended up costing her paying massage clients?

    A. *Massage: One More Thing You Can Do at Home*

    B. *How to Massage Yourself for Fun and Profit*

    C. *Massage Yourself at Home*

427 Why did Chandler's secretary need two weeks off?

    A. She was having one of her boobs reduced.

    B. Her macaw was having molting problems.

    C. Her prosthetic foot came in and she had to have it
       installed.

428 What was Ross's "Carol's in labor" beeper number?

429 After Chandler got promoted, his coworkers (and former friends) called him names behind his back. Which of
the following names did they call him?

    A. Mr. Boss Man

    B. Mr. Big

    C. Boss Man Bing

    D. All of the above

430 Who was André and why did Ross keep receiving his
beeper calls?

431 TRUE OR FALSE: Monica's "youthful" date Ethan told
Monica that until he was nine he thought "gunpoint" was an
actual place.

432 After Monica had sex with Ethan and learned his true
age, she told him that she was now like a certain older

actress who fancies younger men. What actress did Monica mention?

   A. Elizabeth Taylor

   B. Joan Collins

   C. Roseanne

433 What Paul McCartney/Stevie Wonder song did Chandler and Tracy perform during a Karaoke session at an office birthday party?

434 TRUE OR FALSE: Rachel never ended up having a sex dream about Ross.

435 What food item did Joey bring with him when he accompanied Ross to the hospital for the birth of his little Ben?

   A. A dish of ravioli

   B. A bag of Funyuns

   C. A sandwich

EPISODE 23
"The One With the Birth"

FRIEND FACTS: In this humorous, touching (and busy!) episode, Ross, Carol, and Susan all have a son, with a little help from the rest of the bunch; Joey lends a hand when a single girl prepares to give birth and the father is nowhere to be found; Phoebe serenades the hospital waiting room as well as a broom closet's "captive audience"; Monica realizes just how much she wants to have a baby of her own; Rachel shamelessly hits on Carol's OB/GYN; Susan and Ross improbably bond over an innocent pair of coveralls; and Chandler proposes marriage to Monica.

FAVORITE MOMENTS: The birth of Ben is a funny and warm scene, made more so by Ross's astonished, play-by-play description of the actual birth. The funniest moment in this delivery room scene is when Ross gets in the doctor's way by sticking his head down between Carol's legs to get a better look and the doctor says, "Hello?"

436 What kind of candy bar did Susan buy at the hospital gift shop?
   A. Three Musketeers
   B. Milky Way
   C. Chunky

437 What was Carol talking about when she said, "I love them. Each one's like a little party in my uterus"?

438 Chandler promised Monica that if the two of them were still single by a certain age, then *he'd* marry her so she could have a baby of her own. What was Chandler's "marriage cutoff" age?
   A. thirty
   B. forty
   C. fifty

439 Much to Ross's surprise, Susan called his unborn son a name which he had not agreed to. What name did she call Ben?
   A. Jamie
   B. Dylan
   C. Jordy

440 Who ended up locked in the broom closet while Carol was in labor?

   A. Ross, Susan, and Phoebe

   B. Chandler, Monica, and Ross

   C. Joey, Susan, and Phoebe

441 Who is Helper Guy?

442 What did Ross reply when Susan complained that "There's Father's Day, there's Mother's Day, there's no Lesbian Lover Day!"?

443 Who is Hospital Worker Ben?

444 The first time Phoebe saw Ben, she exclaimed that he looked just like one of his *three* parents. Whom did Phoebe think Ben looked like?

   A. Ross

   B. Carol

   C. Susan

445 TRUE OR FALSE: Joey didn't believe that "Ben" was Ben's real name because he didn't answer to it when called.

EPISODE 24
"The One Where Rachel Finds Out"

FRIEND FACTS: In this cliff-hanger season finale (reportedly the first draft script of this episode actually concluded with the words "To Be Continued"), Ross leaves for a trip to China during a birthday barbecue for Rachel; Chandler spills the beans about Ross's feelings for the fetching Ms. Green; Joey participates in a fertility study and learns how to be "generous" in bed; Phoebe channels Ross through a picture; Ross brings home a little "surprise" from China; and there are fruit baskets for everyone!

FAVORITE MOMENTS: I have two favorite scenes in this episode
and they both involve the guys. The first is when Joey and
Chandler burst into Monica's apartment for the barbecue,
armed with charcoal and cooking utensils. "Men are here,"
Chandler announces, followed by Joey, who informs the girls,
"We make fire. Cook meat." My second favorite scene is
when Chandler inadvertently reveals to Rachel that Ross is
in love with her and, for what might actually be the first time
in his life, the loquacious Mr. Bing is at a loss for words!

446 What organization sponsored the fertility study in
which Joey participated?
   A. Columbia Med School
   B. NYU Med School
   C. The Community Reproductive Clinic

447 How long was Joey's fertility study and how much was
he paid at the end of the program?
   A. One week; $100
   B. Two weeks; $700
   C. One month; $1,000

448 What "musical group" did Chandler mention when
Ross asked him if he knew who Carl was?
   A. Paul Revere and the Raiders
   B. Gary Lewis and the Playboys
   C. Alvin and the Chipmunks

449 What was the name of Melanie's fruit basket business?
   A. Bunches of Baskets
   B. The Three Basketeers
   C. Boy O Boy Baskets!

450 Which Dr. Seuss book did Joey give Rachel for her birthday?

    A. *The Cat in the Hat*

    B. *Oh, the Places You'll Go!*

    C. *Daisy Head Mazie*

451 What was the memorable gift Ross left for Rachel, and why was it so special?

452 What was Ross listening to on his cassette player when he boarded the plane to China?

    A. A Chinese language instructional tape

    B. *Hendrix at Monterey*

    C. The Rembrandts' album, *LP*

453 Joey had a giant lit-up replica of a New York City landmark in his bedroom. What was it?

    A. The Statue of Liberty

    B. The United Nations

    C. The Empire State Building

454 TOUGH ONE: What was Ross's China return flight gate number?

    A. 15A

    B. 27B

    C. 33C

455 FOR CREDIT WATCHERS ONLY: What was the name of the Chinese girl Ross brought back from China to meet his friends?

Part 4

The Foosball Room

Monica's Head Chef "audition." Left to right: Jennifer Aniston, Lisa Kudrow, guest star Jon Lovitz, and Courteney Cox.

The *Friends*
Ultimate Pop Culture Matching Test

This test is a little something different. This forty-five-question matching test asks you to match the forty-five pop culture people, places, or things mentioned in the first season of *Friends* from the left column, with the twenty-four *Friends* characters from the right column who are most closely associated with that item.

For example: In one episode, Ross mentions the song "Billy, Don't Be a Hero." If you found that song title in the left column, you would match it with Ross's letter from the right column. Simple, right? This test is terrific fun and will tell you whether or not you need to pay more attention to the particulars of our Friends' world!

Let the matching begin!

456 Gummy Bears	A.	Alan, Monica's date
457 Joan Collins	B.	Carol, Ross's ex-wife
458 James Michener	C.	Chandler Bing
459 ATM Machines	D.	David the Physicist Guy
460 Alvin & the Chipmunks	E.	Fake Monica
461 Football phones	F.	Janice, Chandler's repeat girlfriend
462 The Thighmaster	G.	Jill Goodacre, übermodel
463 Sting	H.	Joey Tribbiani
464 The Weebles Play Palace	I.	Joey Tribbiani Sr.
465 Male escorts	J.	Marcel, Ross's monkey
466 David Hasselhoff	K.	Melanie, Joey's date

467 The Grinch

468 Rocky & Bullwinkle

469 Aromatherapy

470 Dairy Queen

471 "Memories"

472 Candy hearts

473 Pictionary

474 Daryl Hannah

475 Chunky

476 Al Pacino

477 The Heimlich Maneuver

478 Romance novels

479 The Foot Massager

480 *Silence of the Lambs*

481 *Popular Mechanics*

482 Chanel

483 Ships in bottles

484 The Three Musketeers

485 Huey Lewis & the News

486 Travel Scrabble

487 Aramis

488 *An Officer and a Gentleman*

L. Mindy, Rachel's almost maid of honor

M. Monica Geller

N. Mrs. Bing, Chandler's mother

O. Mrs. Tribbiani, Joey's mother

P. Paolo, Rachel's Italian lover

Q. Phoebe Buffay

R. Rachel Green

S. Roger the Psychiatrist

T. Ronni Rappalano; Joey Sr.'s "Date"

U. Ross Geller

V. Steve the Restaurateur

W. Susan, Carol's life partner

X. Ugly naked guy

489 "The Lion Sleeps
         Tonight"
490 Pet mortuaries
491 Funyuns
492 Sweet & Low
493 The San Diego Zoo
494 ... *And Justice for All*
495 The Poconos
496 Fruit baskets
497 *Cycling* magazine
498 Etch-A-Sketch
499 Nicotine patches
500 Hospital gift shops

The Last Question

As all of us *Friends*aholics know, *Friends'* first season made television history. Not since the phenomenal debut of *Charlie's Angels* back in the seventies has a first season series garnered such reviews, such attention, and so many viewers.

Thus, this "Last Question" addresses the incredible success of this terrific show.

501 *Friends* debuted on September 22, 1994, and aired twenty-four episodes in the 1994–95 TV season. What was its final ranking in the Nielsen ratings for this season?

The *Friends*
Character Word Search Puzzle

The following clues will help you find the words in the *Friends* Word Search puzzle. (The word in **BOLD ALL CAPS** is the word you need to look for in the puzzle.)

MONICA Geller

ROSS Geller

RACHEL Green

CHANDLER Bing

PHOEBE Buffay

JOEY Tribbiani

Central **PERK**

MARCEL the Monkey

NBC, *Friends*'s home network

Friends is on at 8:00 on **THURSDAY** night

CAROL, Ross's ex-wife

SUSAN, Carol's "life partner"

BARRY, Rachel's ex-fiancé

MINDY, "Mrs. Barry Farber, DDS"

PAOLO the Italian

URSULA, Phoebe's sister

JANICE, Chandler's recurrent girlfriend

Monica and Ross's dad, **JACK** Geller

Rachel's middle name is **KAREN**

```
J  C  V  L  Z  K  T  F  A  B  K  O  E  R  L
Y  I  A  N  X  P  P  N  S  A  C  C  A  C  V
F  V  C  R  O  M  A  H  R  X  I  C  Z  G  P
Z  V  Q  P  O  U  G  E  G  N  H  A  M  H  O
D  F  V  R  C  L  N  T  A  E  C  U  W  J  Q
P  C  E  H  J  H  H  J  L  I  D  D  W  E  D
Y  E  U  F  L  U  A  M  B  A  Y  W  E  A  X
Y  I  Z  A  R  A  B  N  A  E  L  D  L  J  C
E  J  W  S  C  A  B  J  D  R  B  U  N  Z  B
O  V  D  I  R  Z  M  R  R  L  C  E  S  I  N
J  A  N  R  Q  H  E  H  I  X  E  E  O  R  M
Y  O  Y  E  F  E  P  Q  I  Y  U  R  L  H  U
M  I  P  C  J  A  G  J  F  P  K  C  A  J  P
P  E  R  K  I  D  Y  X  Z  Z  O  L  O  A  P
S  U  S  A  N  J  J  F  W  H  D  S  S  O  R
```

BARRY	MARCEL	PHOEBE
CAROL	MINDY	RACHEL
CHANDLER	MONICA	ROSS
JACK	NBC	SUSAN
JANICE	PAOLO	THURSDAY
JOEY	PERK	URSULA
KAREN		

EXTRAS

Friends Cast Credits

The Friends

Jennifer Aniston	Rachel Green
Courteney Cox	Monica Geller
Lisa Kudrow	Phoebe Buffay
Matt LeBlanc	Joey Tribbiani
Matthew Perry	Chandler Bing
David Schwimmer	Ross Geller

Supporting Cast

[NOTE: **Bold** indicates recurring character]

Jay Acovone	Fireman Charlie
Jack Armstrong	Bob
Anita Barone	**Carol Willick (1), Ross's ex-wife**
Tommy Blaze	Carl
Corinne Bohrer	Melanie
Jackie Bright	The janitor
Leesa Bryte	Leslie
Brian Buckner	Office worker #2
Fritzi Burr	Ms. Tedlock
Nancy Cassaro	Shelly
Megan Cavanaugh	Luisa Gianetti
Benjamin Caya	Bratty boy
Lynn Clark	Danielle

120

Stuart Fratkin	Lowell
Cosimo Fusco	**Paolo, Rachel's Italian lover**
June Gable	The delivery nurse
Beverly Garland	Aunt Iris
Lee Garlington	Ronni Rappalano; Joey Sr.'s Mistress
Kim Gillingham	Angela
Mary Pat Gleason	Nurse Dora Sizemore
Beth Grant	Lizzy
Jennifer Grant	Nina Bookbinder
Joel Gretsch	Fireman Ed
Marianne Hagan	Joanne
Alaina Reed Hall	The admissions woman
Larry Hankin	**Mr. Heckles [originally "The Weird Man"]**
Melora Hardin	Celia
Lara Harris	The Obsession girl
Jessica Hecht	**Susan Bunch, Carol's partner**
Carlo Imperato	Roy
Stan Kirsch	Ethan
Kerrie Klark	Flight representative
Lisa Kudrow	**Ursula [from *Mad About You*]**
Clea Lewis	**Franny**
Jenifer Lewis	Paula
Geoffrey Lower	Alan
Carolyn Lowery	Andrea
Sarah MacDonnell	Sandy
Michele Maika	Kiki
Cynthia Mann	Jasmine
Cynthia Mann	The waitress
Heather Medway	Kristen Riggs
Sofia Milos	Aurora
Christopher Miranda	Bobby
Christopher Miranda	Robbie
John Allen Nelson	Paul the Wine Guy

Jo Jean Pagano	Customer
Wayne Péré	Max the Scientist Geek
Christina Pickles	**Judy Geller, Ross and Monica's mom**
Larry Poindexter	Fireman Dave
Joan Pringle	Dr. Oberman
Leah Remini	Lydia
Michele Lamar Richards	The Lamaze teacher
Jack Riley	Airline passenger
Camille Saviola	The Horrible Woman
David Sederholm	Coma guy
Claudia Shear	Fake Monica
Jane Sibbett	**Carol Willick (2), Ross's ex-wife**
Darryl Sivad	Office worker #3
Elisabeth Sjoli	Tia
Philip Rayburn Smith	The actor
Karla Tamburelli	The teacher
Patty Tiffany	Woman
Marilyn Tokuda	Nurse
Lauren Tom	**Julie**
Nancy Valen	Lorraine
Vincent Ventresca	Fun Bobby
Angela Visser	Samantha
Sean Whalen	Pizza Guy
Maggie Wheeler	**Janice, Chandler's girlfriend**
Mitchell Whitfield	**Barry Farber**
Dorien Wilson	Mr. Douglas, Chandler's boss
Max Wright	Terry

Celebrity Guest Stars

Hank Azaria	David the Physicist Guy
George Clooney	Dr. Michael Mitchell, ER doctor
Jill Connick	Jill Goodacre, Übermodel

Robert Costanzo	Joey Tribbiani Sr., Joey's dad
Elinor Donahue	Aunt Lillian (Ross and Monica's)
Morgan Fairchild	Nora Tyler Bing, Chandler's mom
Elliott Gould	**Jack Geller, Ross and Monica's dad**
Jennifer Grey	Mindy, Barry's fiancé
Helen Hunt	Jamie Buchman [from *Mad About You*]
Leila Kenzle	Fran Devanow [from *Mad About You*]
Jay Leno	Himself
Jon Lovitz	Steve the Restaurateur
Merrill Markoe	Marsha the Museum Curator
Harry Shearer	Dr. Baldharar, Animal "Fight Promoter"
Jonathan Silverman	Dr. Franzblau, Carol's OB/GYN
Fisher Stevens	Roger the Psychiatrist
Brenda Vaccaro	Gloria Tribbiani, Joey's mom
Noah Wyle	Dr. Jeffrey Rosen, ER doctor

Must See Thursdays: The Original Air Dates of *Friends* Legendary Debut Season

September 22, 1994–May 18, 1995

Episode Number and Title	Original Air Date
1. "The One Where Monica Geta a Roommate" [Pilot]	9/22/94
2. "The One With the Sonogram at the End"	9/29/94
3. "The One With the Thumb"	10/06/94
4. "The One With George Stephanopoulos"	10/13/94
5. "The One With the East German Laundry Detergent"	10/20/94
6. "The One With the Butt"	10/27/94

7.	"The One With the Blackout"	11/03/94
8.	"The One Where Nana Dies Twice"	11/10/94
9.	"The One Where Underdog Gets Away"	11/17/94
10.	"The One With the Monkey"	12/15/94
11.	"The One With Mrs. Bing"	1/05/95
12.	"The One With the Dozen Lasagnas"	1/12/95
13.	"The One With the Boobies"	1/19/95
14.	"The One With the Candy Hearts"	2/09/95
15.	"The One With the Stoned Guy"	2/16/95
16.	"The One With Two Parts" Part 1	2/23/95
17.	"The One With Two Parts" Part 2	2/23/95
18.	"The One With All the Poker"	3/02/95
19.	"The One Where the Monkey Gets Away"	3/09/95
20.	"The One With the Evil Orthodontist"	4/06/95
21.	"The One With Fake Monica"	4/27/95
22.	"The One With the Ick Factor"	5/04/95
23.	"The One With the Birth"	5/11/95
24.	"The One Where Rachel Finds Out" [Season Finale]	5/18/95

The Brains Behind *Friends*: The Writers and Directors

These two charts provide, at a glance, all the writers and directors of *Friends* amazing first season. The writers and directors are provided in chronological order, beginning with the first episode. (*Friends* was created by Marta Kauffman and David Crane.)

[NOTE: To save space, the title words "The One With . . . " or "The One Where . . . " (which is how all the titles begin) have been eliminated from the charts. Complete listings of the episode titles appear elsewhere several times throughout this volume.]

Writer(s)	Episode Titles
Marta Kauffman/David Crane	"Monica Gets a Roommate"; "The Sonogram at the End"; "Nana Dies Twice"; "Two Parts" Parts 1 and 2; "The Birth" [story only]
Jeffrey Astrof/Mike Sikowitz	"The Thumb"; "The Blackout"; "All the Poker"; "The Monkey Gets Away"
Alexa Junge	"George Stephanopoulos"; "Mrs. Bing"; "The Boobies"; "The Ick Factor"
Jeff Greenstein/Jeff Straus	"The East German Laundry Detergent"; "Underdog Gets Away"; "The Stoned Guy"; "The Birth" [teleplay only]
Adam Chase/Ira Ungerleider	"The Butt"; "The Monkey"; "Fake Monica"
Bill Lawrence	"The Candy Hearts"
Doty Abrams	"The Evil Orthodontist"
Chris Brown	"Rachel Finds Out"
Jeffrey Astrof/Mike Sikowitz and Adam Chase/ Ira Ungerleider	"The Dozen Lasagnas"

Director	Episode Titles
James Burrows	"Monica Gets a Roommate"; "The Sonogram at the End"; "The Thumb"; "George Stephanopoulos"; "The Blackout"; "Nana Dies Twice"; "Underdog Gets Away"; "Mrs. Bing"; "The Candy Hearts"; "All The Poker"; "The Birth"
Pamela Fryman	"The East German Laundry Detergent"
Arlene Sanford	"The Butt"
Peter Bonerz	"The Monkey"; "The Monkey Gets Away"; "The Evil Orthodontist"
Paul Lazarus	"The Dozen Lasagnas"
Alan Myerson	"The Boobies"; "The Stoned Guy"
Michael Lembeck	"Two Parts" Parts 1 and 2
Gail Mancuso	"Fake Monica"
Robby Benson	"The Ick Factor"
Kevin S. Bright	"Rachel Finds Out"

ANSWERS

Friends Fundamentals

1 A, 3; B, 1; C, 4; D, 2
2 Lincoln High
3 Two
4 B
5 Because, doy, he was ugly and he was always naked. (With thanks to Phoebe for the "doy.")
6 A, B, C, D, E, F, and G
7 C
8 B
9 Central Perk
10 A
11 B
12 C
13 A
14 True
15 A
16 B
17 A
18 A
19 C
20 True
21 B
22 A
23 C
24 B
25 C
26 True

27 C

28 By climbing out a window.

29 A

30 True

31 C

32 True

33 B. (This was part of the fabricated story she created in an attempt to trap Fake Monica.)

34 True. (Ross, Joey, and Rachel used these new appliances as an excuse to leave Monica and Ethan alone when the high-schooler came to see Monica at the coffeehouse.)

35 Rachel. (This is how she introduced herself to Dr. Franzblau while Carol was in labor.)

Chandler Bing

36 He was nine, and they told him at Thanksgiving dinner. (In "The One With the Boobies," Roger the Creepy Psychiatrist Guy told Chandler that his parents divorcing before he hit puberty and him ending up being a chronic joker was "textbook.")

37 True. As of their Valentine's Day blind date he had dumped her twice. His post-dinner dump made three times.

38 A

39 Weekly Estimated Net Usage Statistics.

40 C

41 True

42 A

43 "lesbian"

44 C

45 True

46 B

47 Hannibal Lecter. (He told Ross, "I thought you were great in *The Silence of the Lambs*.")

48 C

49 True. He thought this deed quite brave.

50 C

51 B

52 C

53 Chandler's boss.

54 A

55 7143457

56 True

57 A

58 A

59 True

60 C

61 True

62 B

63 C

64 A

65 He kept rubbing his temples and Joey told him, "That's good. Just keep rubbing your head. That'll turn back time."

Phoebe Buffay

66 C

67 A

68 A

69 True

70 B

71 True

72 Yellow

73 Ursula

74 B

75 B

76 C

77 True

78 A
79 B
80 C
81 True
82 B
83 True
84 A
85 True
86 "homosexual"
87 B
88 True
89 B
90 Nintendo Gameboy
91 "sweet"; "resent"
92 D
93 A
94 B
95 C

Monica Geller

96 E
97 False
98 C. (After it was over and the dust had settled, Phoebe told Rachel, "I can't believe you tried to move the green ottoman!")
99 "Our Little Harmonica."
100 A
101 B
102 C
103 True. (When she showed the picture to Phoebe and Rachel, Rachel commented. "He's wearing a sweater," to which Monica replied, "Nooo." They then all "Ewwwww"ed.)
104 False. She was fat in high school.

105 A

106 He could belch it. (The alphabet, that is.)

107 D

108 False! Ross remembered that Monica's Raggedy Ann was the only one that *wasn't* raggedy.

109 D

110 C

111 C

112 Because a woman passed by holding a brand new baby. (Chandler had to rescue Monica by making fake static noises into the phone and then hanging up on her mother.)

113 A

114 C

115 A

116 Manana

117 B

118 False. Mon did *not* like *Mrs. Doubtfire*.

119 C

120 A

121 A

122 She suggested that he be there "for her." (Melanie, his new girlfriend.) He didn't get it.

123 C

124 She was talking about what it would be like if Rachel decided to date her (Monica's) brother Ross.

125 B

Ross Geller

126 B

127 A

128 C

129 He wanted his tablemates at the Japanese restaurant to slide down (scooching) so he could sit with Carol.

130 A

131 C

132 False. He wore a quartz watch.

133 B

134 True

135 B

136 Rachel *Green*

137 A

138 True

139 C

140 False. ChiChi died, but his parents told him the farm story so as not to upset him.

141 B

142 False. Ross absolutely could *not* sleep in a public place.

143 B

144 False. Carol wore boots that night and never took them off (although the part about the major turn-on is probably true).

145 B

146 False. Ross's fabric softener of choice was usually Snuggles. (He skipped the Snuggles when he and Rachel went on a "laundry date.")

147 A

148 Being buried alive. This fear was realized when he fell into an open grave while walking through the cemetery after Nana's funeral.

149 "uterus"

150 C

151 James Michener

152 She believed that The Flintstones could have really happened.

153 C

154 "big bone"

155 C

Rachel Green

156 True

157 Her best friend and almost maid of honor, Mindy.

158 B

159 Karen

160 True

161 C. (When she asked, "Did I just share too much?" after revealing this, Ross replied, "Just a smidge.")

162 False. She had *no* medical insurance, necessitating the identity switch with Monica in the second half of the two-part episode, "The One With Two Parts."

163 B

164 True

165 A

166 C

167 B

168 True

169 A

170 On heaving beasts. (On page 2 of her romance novel *A Woman Undone*, Rachel wrote about "heaving beasts," "niffles," and "his huge throbbing pens.")

171 B

172 C

173 A

174 True (according to her typo-riddled resume, that is).

175 C

176 False. She was actually quite good and in the tap class with Monica, Fake Monica, and Phoebe, she surprised them all by how talented she was.

177 B. (Chandler explained to Rachel that you kind of had to "pick your moments.")

178 A

179 C

180 Ed Begley Jr.

181 A

182 C. (He shouted this because he was the bigmouth who told her about Ross.)

183 False. The flight representative gave the message to some guy instead of Ross.

184 B

185 A

Joey Tribbiani

186 C

187 C

188 False. Joey liked nudity in his movies. A lot.

189 A and B. ("Nothing that spatters.")

190 True

191 C

192 B

193 C

194 False. He said he didn't know if he'd ever been in love and his father then explained that that meant he hadn't.

195 B

196 To keep her off the balcony where Ross was attempting to tell Rachel the truth about his feelings for her.

197 A

198 False. Phoebe blurted out this fact during the blackout (as she was complaining that she was always the last to know everything).

199 A. (He was one of seven children.)

200 Dr. Bazzita

201 D

202 C

203 "Or an uncle."

204 B

205 False. The Tribbianis are Roman Catholic.

206 A

207 B

208 C

209 A

210 B

211 C

212 "hooker"; "stomach"; "fat"; "sores"; "face"

213 *The Unbearable Lightness of Being*

214 B

215 She was referring to his participation in a fertility study which required him to make sperm donations every other day for two weeks.

(1) "The One Where Monica Gets a Roommate"

216 C

217 A

218 B

219 A

220 They were watching the soap opera with the Spanish language soundtrack instead of the English one.

221 "La, la, something with string"

222 C

223 A, 2; B, 2; C, 2; D, 1; E, 1

224 True

225 B

(2) "The One With the Sonogram at the End"

226 B

227 A

228 B

229 C. (Monica was nervous about having her parents over for dinner.)

230 B

231 A

232 B

233 A. (Her mother remarked, "*That's* easy," when told what they would be eating.)

234 Dr. Oberman

235 A, B, and C

(3) "The One With the Thumb"

236 A

237 A, 3; B, 1; C, 4; D, 2

238 B

239 "Not mine, not mine, not mine."

240 "Not-not mine, not-not mine, not-not mine."

241 C

242 "For a while."

243 B

244 C

245 A, 6; B, 3; C, 1; D, 5; E, 2; F, 4

(4) "The One With George Stephanopoulos"

246 A, 1; B, 2; C, 1 and 3; D, 1; E, 4; F, 1 (Ross jokingly told Phoebe that she had picked *his* wish when she asked for bigger boobs, and Joey thought "omnipotent" meant "impotent." Also, Monica and Rachel didn't participate: Their names were included as a decoy!)

247 C

248 "To hell with hockey! Let's *all* do that!"

249 B

250 B

251 A and C. (Although Phoebe lost the "Operation" tweezers so all they could do was prep the guy.)

252 C

253 A

254 False. That's the pie that George Stephanopoulos ordered and which the girls got by mistake. Their pizza was supposed to be fat-free crust with extra cheese.

255 A, 3; B, 1; C, 2; D, 2

(5) "The One With the East German Laundry Detergent"

256 A, 3; B, 1; C, 2; D, 4; E, 4

257 B

258 C

259 A

260 B

261 C. (He already had Rocky socks. Now he could mix and match: "Moose and squirrel.")

262 C

263 True. (Supposedly. Although what's probably closer to the truth is that Joey deliberately mentioned this little habit just to turn off Angela's new date Bob.)

264 A

265 C

(6) "The One With the Butt"

266 "dingle"; "schvang"; "tinkle"

267 The exclamation point in the title scared her.

268 A

269 A. (Rick was her husband; while Ethan, Andrew, and, of course, Chandler, were all her lovers.)

270 B
271 B
272 A
273 C
274 A
275 A

(7) "The One With the Blackout"

276 It was a vestibule: "Jill says vestibule. I'm going with vestibule."
277 C
278 A, 5; B, 2; C, 1; D, 3; E, 4
279 B. (This was Joey's way of explaining to Ross that he waited too long to make his movie on Rachel and now he was in The Friend Zone.)
280 "sour"; "dairy"
281 A
282 "perfection"
283 B
284 A
285 "Crapweasel"

(8) "The One Where Nana Dies Twice"

286 C
287 B
288 A
289 B
290 B
291 True
292 C
293 B

294 B
295 C

(9) "The One Where Underdog Gets Away"

296 B
297 C
298 A
299 Being a lesbian.
300 B. (That's how Carol and Susan referred to Ross when they spoke to the unborn baby through Carol's belly.)
301 A
302 Mario
303 "bagel"; "zoo"; "breasts"
304 A. (This was Rachel's nickname for the eloquent Mr. Bing.)
305 C

(10) "The One With the Monkey"

306 A. (This was Ross's lame attempt to cover his faux pas of describing having a roommate as "pathetic.")
307 "dead in the kitchen"
308 David the Scientist Guy and his colleague Max the Physicist Guy. (Phoebe called them "Noisy Boys" when they talked too loudly during one of her performances.)
309 B
310 A
311 C
312 B
313 True. (Ross was stunned to learn that his monkey had performed this trick for Chandler when Ross was away.)
314 A
315 Joey

(11) "The One With Mrs. Bing"

316 B

317 C

318 D. (*A Woman Undone* was the title of *Rachel's* novel. All the others are actual Nora Bing books.)

319 B

320 A, 1; B, 1; C, 2; D, 1; E, 2; F, 2; G, 1

321 C

322 B

323 A

324 A

325 Yes. (This was a question Rachel asked Monica as she was writing her romance novel. Monica assured her that it could, indeed, be liberated in such a manner.)

(12) "The One With the Dozen Lasagnas"

326 C

327 A

328 False. He definitely did *not* want to know.

329 C

330 A

331 True

332 A

333 C, after his pass at Phoebe was revealed.

334 Ross. This was the role that Joey and Chandler envisioned for Ross as they encouraged him to jump in and make a move on Rachel after Paolo cheated on her. (They wanted him to usher in "The Age of Ross.")

335 A

(13) "The One With the Boobies"

336 "nippular"

337 Sparky is the name Chandler called Roger after the shrink told the ever-joking Chandler that he wouldn't want to be there when the laughter stops.

338 A and B

339 C

340 B

341 C

342 Kicky is the name Chandler called Joey when they had to share a bed and Joey kept kicking the covers off. (They slept together because Joey's dad and his dad's girlfriend were visiting.)

343 True

344 C

345 True

(14) "The One With the Candy Hearts"

346 B

347 A

348 C. (When she demonstrated this particular "skill" to Joey under the restaurant table, Joey asked her, "Quarters? Or *rolls* of quarters?")

349 A

350 B

351 C

352 "The semen of a righteous man."

353 B

354 Three; Fireman Ed, Fireman Dave, and Fireman Charlie. (The girls ended up wearing their hats.)

355 A

(15) "The One With the Stoned Guy"

356 B. (This is the name Phoebe called Chandler when she saw him all dressed up on his way to see his career counselor.)

357 A

358 A

359 D

360 C

361 B

362 B

363 Rachel. (This is what Steve called her when she answered the door to the apartment the night of Monica's "audition.")

364 He said, "Well, smack my ass and call me Judy!"

365 E

(16) "The One With Two Parts" Part 1

366 True. (And he did it a lot, too.)

367 A, E, and F

368 E

369 Rachel

370 B

371 A. (This was a very important number to Chandler because his A.N.U.S. hinged on his W.E.N.U.S.)

372 False. (But as he told Monica, he "*could* have cats.")

373 C

374 A

375 B

(17) "The One With Two Parts"
Part 2

376 A

377 C. (He dropped it when the guests all yelled "surprise!" at him and he was startled.)

378 B

379 C

380 A, 2; B, 1; C, 2; D, 1; E, 2; F, 3; H, 2

381 B

382 A

383 forty-three

384 He swallowed a "K," an "M," and an "O" and Chandler guessed he was trying to spell "monkey."

385 B

(18) "The One With All the Poker"

386 C

387 A

388 True. (This came up when Chandler asked Ross, "Could you want her anymore?," speaking, of course, about Ross's love for Rachel. When a distracted Ross replied, "Who?," Chandler said, "Dee, the sarcastic sister on *What's Happening!*")

389 B

390 C

391 C

392 A

393 B

394 B

395 "see"; "fly's"; "look"

(19) "The One Where the Monkey Gets Away"

396 A

397 'Pee in the'

398 C

399 A, 2; B, 1

400 C

401 B

402 A

403 B

404 C

405 Patty was really Marcel the monkey. "Patty" was the phony name Mr. Heckles gave the monkey when he "monkey-napped" him. (Marcel was wearing a pink dress when they finally found him.)

(20) "The One With the Evil Orthodontist"

406 True

407 C. (He already had a Thighmaster.)

408 San Francisco

409 C

410 A

411 Mindy

412 B

413 "Ring, dammit! Ring!" (But he was talking about his phone, not Ross's crossword puzzle answer!)

414 True

415 C

(21) "The One With Fake Monica"

416 D

417 C

418 C

419 Who else? The *real* Monica.

420 A. (He got in, too)

421 "Take off their hats!"

422 C

423 True

424 A

425 B

(22) "The One With the Ick Factor"

426 C

427 A

428 55-JIMBO

429 D

430 André was a male outcall guy whose beeper number was 55-*JUMBO*.

431 True

432 B. (Ethan had never heard of her.)

433 "Ebony and Ivory"

434 Apparently False. Ross heard her moan his name while she was sleeping but just when he was going to tell her his true feelings for her, his "Carol's in labor" beeper went off.

435 C

(23) "The One With the Birth"

436 C

437 Her labor contractions

438 B

439 C

440 A

441 Joey. ("Helper Guy" is the way Lydia described Joey on the phone to Roy, the father of her baby.)

442 "*Every* day is Lesbian Lover Day!"

443 Phoebe, after she put on Ben's coveralls to climb up into the ceiling of the broom closet where she, Ross, and Susan were trapped to see if she could find a way out. This is where Ross came up with the name "Ben" for his son.

444 C

445 Amazing, but True.

(24) "The One Where Rachel Finds Out"

446 B

447 B

448 C

449 B

450 B

451 He left her a cameo brooch that the two of them had seen in an antique store months earlier. Rachel had mentioned to him that her grandmother had had one just like it and Ross had remembered.

452 A

453 C

454 B

455 Julie. (She was played by Lauren Tom and her name was not mentioned in the episode.)

The Friends Ultimate Pop Culture Matching Test

456,V; **457**,M; **458**,U; **459**,G; **460**,C; **461**,Q; **462**,X; **463**,O; **464**,S; **465**,U; **466**,A; **467**,C; **468**,F; **469**,Q; **470**,Q; **471**,E; **472**,F; **473**,M;

474,D; **475**,W; **476**,H; **477**,G; **478**,N; **479**,M; **480**,U; **481**,R; **482**,L; **483**,I; **484**,K; **485**,B; **486**,R; **487**,H; **488**,Q; **489**,J; **490**,T; **491**,C; **492**,R; **493**,J; **494**,H; **495**,P; **496**,H; **497**,U; **498**,M; **499**,C; **500**,W

The Last Question

501 *Friends* finished as the eighth most watched show in America for the 1994–1995 television season. (It was beaten only by *NYPD Blue*, *60 Minutes*, *Monday Night Football*, *Grace Under Fire*, *Home Improvement*, *ER*, and at number 1, *Seinfeld*. *ER* and *Friends* were the only *new* shows to finish in the Top Ten.)

The *Friends* Character Word Search Puzzle Answers

J	C	V	L	Z	K	T	F	A	B	K	O	E	R	L
Y	I	A	N	X	P	P	N	S	A	C	C	A	C	V
F	V	C	R	O	M	A	H	R	X	I	C	Z	G	P
Z	V	Q	P	O	U	G	E	G	N	H	A	M	H	O
D	F	V	R	C	L	N	T	A	E	C	U	W	J	Q
P	C	E	H	J	H	H	J	L	I	D	D	W	E	D
Y	E	U	F	L	U	A	M	B	A	Y	W	E	A	X
Y	I	Z	A	R	A	B	N	A	E	L	D	L	J	C
E	J	W	S	C	A	B	J	D	R	B	U	N	Z	B
O	V	D	I	R	Z	M	R	R	L	C	E	S	I	N
J	A	N	R	Q	H	E	H	I	X	E	E	O	R	M
Y	O	Y	E	F	E	P	Q	I	Y	U	R	L	H	U
M	I	P	C	J	A	G	J	F	P	K	C	A	J	P
P	E	R	K	I	D	Y	X	Z	Z	O	L	O	A	P
S	U	S	A	N	J	J	F	W	H	D	S	S	O	R

About the Author

STEPHEN J. SPIGNESI is a writer who specializes in popular culture subjects, including television, film, and contemporary fiction. His other books include:

- *Mayberry, My Hometown* (Popular Culture, Ink.)
- *The Complete Stephen King Encyclopedia* (Popular Culture, Ink; Contemporary Books)
- *The Stephen King Quiz Book* (Signet)
- *The Second Stephen King Quiz Book* (Signet)
- *The Woody Allen Companion* (Andrews and McMeel; Plexus; Popular Culture, Ink)
- *The Official "Gone With the Wind" Companion* (Plume)
- *The V.C. Andrews Trivia and Quiz Book* (Signet)
- *The Odd Index: The Ultimate Compendium of Bizarre and Unusual Facts* (Plume)
- *What's Your "Mad About You" I.Q.?* (Citadel Press)
- *The Gore Galore Video Quiz Book* (Signet)
- *The Celebrity Baby Name Book* (forthcoming, Signet)
- *The Italian 100: A Ranking of the Most Influential Italians, Past and Present* (forthcoming, Citadel Press)
- *Stephen King A to Z* (forthcoming, Popular Culture, Ink)

In addition to writing, Spignesi also lectures widely on a variety of popular culture subjects and is the founder and editor-in-chief of the small press publishing company, *The Stephen John Press*. He lives in New Haven, Connecticut, with his wife Pam.